CANADIAN GHOST STORIES

Barbara Smith

Illustrations by Arlana Anderson-Hale

LONE
PINE

Lone Pine Publishing

The Publisher: Lone Pine Publishing
10145 – 81 Avenue
Edmonton, AB T6E 1W9
Canada

Website: http://www.lonepinepublishing.com

Canadian Cataloguing in Publication Data
Smith, Barbara, 1947–
    Canadian ghost stories

    ISBN 1-55105-302-0

    1. Ghosts—Canada.   2. Legends—Canada.   I. Title.
GR580.S669 2001   398.2'097105   C00-911591-9

Editorial Director: Nancy Foulds
Project Editor: Shelagh Kubish
Illustrations Coordinator: Carol Woo
Production Manager: Jody Reekie
Book Design: Heather Markham, Arlana Anderson-Hale
Cover Design: Robert Weidemann
Layout & Production: Arlana Anderson-Hale
Illustrations: Arlana Anderson-Hale

Photo Credits: City of Toronto (p. 33); Joanne Rochon family (p. 64); NWT Archives/Fred Jackson/NK-1979-004 (p. 84); Vernon Oickle (p. 124); Glenbow Archives/PD-313-187 (p. 164); Katy Parsons/Lighthouse Publishing (p. 188); Earle Rother (p. 235).

The stories, folklore and legends in this book are based on the author's collection of sources including individuals whose experiences have led them to believe they have encountered phenomena of some kind or another. They are meant to entertain, and neither the publisher nor the author claims these stories represent fact.

We acknowledge the financial support of the Government of Canada through the Book Publishing Industry Development Program (BPIDP) for our publishing activities.

PC: P6

Dedication

This book is dedicated, with love, to my daughter
Robyn, who has travelled across Canada many times.

Contents

Acknowledgements 7

Introduction 9

Chapter 1   Haunted Houses

Location, Location, Location 13

Protective Presence 21

Island Entities 24

Ghostly Helper 26

"Funky" Haunted Apartment 27

Suburban Spirits 29

Haunted Park 32

All in the Family 36

Jumpin' Jammers 41

Patty Cake 49

Fred's Family Phantom 51

Twelve Stranded Men .55

Haunted Honeymoon .59

Murdered Manifestation 61

Old House Haunter 62

Musical Manifestation 66

Welcome Home 70

Chapter 2   Transported to Beyond

Legend of the Light 76
Upsetting Journey 81
Ghostly Smoker 86
On and Off the Road Again 90
Titanic 93
The Voice 102
Regina's Demise 105
Ghostly Presence 107
Spectral Ships 113
The *Young Teazer* .115
Ghost of the Baie 118
Fire Upon the Water 120
Pacific Presences 122
Jane Miller of the Bay 124

Chapter 3   Spirit Snippets 126

Chapter 4   The Spirit's Inn

The Algonquin Hotel 150
Pub "Creepy" Crawlers 153
Spectral Speaker 156
Frontenac Returns .158
Ghost Attends Conference 161
"Maud" Stays Home 162
Haunted Landmark Razed 163
Spirits at the Bar 167

Chapter 5   Historically Haunted

Ghost Brothers 171

Brother from Beyond 175

The Thing 179

Knock, Knock, Who's There? 182

The Real McCoy? 184

Ghostly Chief 185

Evil, Cursed, Haunted or All Three? 187

Chapter 6   They Came Back

Possession by a Poltergeist 195

The Grandfather Clock 206

Close Cousins 207

Caged Spirit 209

Phantom Footsteps 212

Mistaken Identity 214

River Wraith 217

Ghostly Queen 219

"Devil Dog" 222

Lady in Pink 227

Foreign Phantoms? .230

Possessed Plane 233

Laura's Legacy 238

Acknowledgements

As with all my books, I have had a great deal of help in researching, compiling and writing the stories that follow. Because of the nature of the work I do, some people who have helped me have requested anonymity. I respect those wishes but sincerely hope all of you know how appreciative I am of your contributions. Thank you. Another debt of thanks is owed to the people who contributed stories and allowed their names to run.

In addition, there are always those kind few who provide help and support in many ways. Steve Bartlett of Chatham, Ontario, has kept my projects in mind for years and has sent me valuable leads, insights and material. W. Ritchie Benedict of Calgary is certainly the most tenacious paranormal researcher I've ever met—and a very kind and generous one. Long-time friend Jane Chartley, of Moncton, cleverly expedited my access to the cache of ghost stories in eastern Canada. Leslie Charlton of Regina brought Saskatchewan stories to my attention. My fellow ghost story author Jo-Anne Christensen and her husband Dennis Shappka are always a source of the support found in a close friendship, but in addition I was able to tap into their resources and experiences, and this book is stronger for it. Thank you both. Dr. Terry Matheson, professor of English at the University of Saskatchewan in Saskatoon, was most generous in sharing his experiences for this book. My dear friend Dr. Barrie Robinson supported me with his friendship while I wrote this book and also offered and shared with me his considerable editorial skills. Please know that I'm so appreciative. As always, my husband Bob Smith helped in many, usually inherently unrewarding, ways. Thank you, Bob. Bill Turner, host of a phone-in program on CKLQ radio in Brandon, Manitoba, supported my collections by inviting me to be a guest on his show.

There would be no point to anyone's efforts if it were not for the talented, hard-working and friendly people who make up Lone Pine Publishing. Thanks to all and specifically to Shane Kennedy, Nancy Foulds and Shelagh Kubish, as well as Arlana Anderson-Hale for her illustrations.

(Note: "Smith" is a very common name, but as far as I know, I am not related to any of the Smiths mentioned in the following stories.)

Introduction

Some of the most satisfying results of my books of true ghost stories have been the numbers of personal experience stories that readers have sent me. As the anecdotes describing people's supernatural encounters arrived in my office, I read them all, shivered at some, remembered to send my generous correspondent a thank-you note (I hope I didn't forget any!) and then filed the story away for future reference. As a result, when Lone Pine Publishing approached me to write a book of true ghost stories from all across Canada, I was ready and eager to begin the project.

Please remember that the narratives in this book are reports of real events. We all know that life, as we live it, is anything but neat. As a result, these accounts tend to be a bit more ragged than stories we may be used to reading. A fictional tale of a haunting will be structured with a predictable presentation: a beginning, a middle and an end. The incidents recorded here refuse to be that orderly. Sometimes people writing to me about their encounters have been so overwhelmed by their experience that they have not been able to recall all the details. This can, occasionally, leave us with fragments, a possibly frustrating result in a world so fond of tidy resolutions. We tend to find it more satisfying when loose ends are bound up in the last sentence of a tale. Nonetheless, I hope you will find—as I have come to—that in the instances where there isn't enough information to tell a traditional story, the parts that are missing are every bit as provocative as the parts that remain.

The following is a "new" collection of stories, "new" in that none of the stories has been published in this series before. For the most part, they are tales that have been brought to my attention most recently. Each one chosen for inclusion has succeeded in making me firmly believe that we do not and cannot completely understand the world around us.

Is there such a thing as ghosts? Isn't there such a thing as ghosts? I don't think we can ever know for sure. What I do know is that the people who've entrusted me with their stories have had profoundly moving experiences. I also know that I've had a few incidents in my life that I cannot explain. I know that I've seen a lid from a sugar bowl lift off its base, travel through the air and set itself down gently. There were only two people in the room at that time and neither of us was touching either the bowl or its lid. I've seen inexplicable mists, pillars of vapour. I've smelled cigarette smoke where there's been no earthly reason for such an odour to be present. I've sat alone in a hotel room, contemplating how best to tell some ghost stories for which I had a particular fondness, when the light from the bedside lamp simply and mysteriously went out, only to come back on, just as simply and just as mysteriously, a minute or so later.

Am I a believer? Definitely more so than not. I'll admit we may be misnaming the phenomena we're labelling as "ghosts," but that could merely reflect the constant conundrum about language—it both creates and limits our reality.

So, having posed far more questions than you'll find answered in this book, I invite you to dive into the stories. I hope you enjoy them. Let them play with your emotions and your imagination, but most of all I simply hope that you have fun reading the stories I've re-told here. I've certainly enjoyed writing them.

If you have any ghost stories of your own that you'd like to share with me, I'd be pleased to hear from you. You can write to me care of Lone Pine Publishing.

CHAPTER 1

Haunted Houses

*Our homes are extremely important to most of us.
Whether home is a single room in a boarding house,
a ranch, a city bungalow or a condominium
apartment in a downtown high-rise,
we humans tend to develop strong emotional
attachments to our homes. Perhaps, then,
it shouldn't be too surprising that such an intimate,
emotionally laden area is frequently also the site of
paranormal activity.*

*As you will find when you read the following tales,
how homes become haunted and what the
ghostly activity consists of vary as much as
the homes themselves.*

Location, Location, Location

In 1997 Kathy Smith first wrote to me about her family's paranormal experiences in a southeast Edmonton townhouse. I was especially intrigued because I live fairly close to the haunted rental property.

The townhouse the Smiths lived in is part of a development that was built to help ease the housing shortage following the Second World War. The housing units must have been considered quite innovative when they were built, and even today, they retain the look of a unique community and offer a comfortable place to live at a reasonable price. The residences are laid out in clusters of six, surrounded by spacious lawns, and from the outside appear to be identical, each with a basement, a ground floor and a second storey.

The Smiths—Kathy, her husband Gary, and their two-and-a-half-year-old daughter Jackie—moved into the complex in 1992. It wasn't long before Kathy began to suspect that their new accommodations were anything but ordinary.

"Shortly after we moved in to the townhouse ... we began to notice that something was not quite right," Kathy explained, adding that the basement was "especially creepy," and that whenever she went down there to do the laundry she had a distinct impression that she was not alone. "I felt that someone was watching me. There was a large, old furnace to the right of the washer and dryer that I found rather scary-looking on its own and I could 'feel' a presence near it. Almost every time I was near the furnace, I saw, out of the corner of my eye, a dark form which appeared to be standing beside it."

On the few occasions Kathy was able to summon the courage to turn her head and look directly into the area where she'd seen the shape, she "saw nothing."

Despite its apparent shyness about being seen, the presence was not content to stay within its subterranean realm. "Gary had his first encounter with the ghost when, late one night, he heard loud footsteps coming up the basement stairs." Courageously, "he went over and opened the basement door to see who was making the noise ... there was no one there."

The sounds of phantom footsteps are common occurrences in a haunted house, as are random smells and isolated areas of inexplicable cold. The Smiths' townhouse was home to all of these ghostly signs. "There was always a strange odour in the house that we could never get rid of. One day, a smell that was more horrible than anything else I had ever experienced filled the living room. It was so awful that it made me nauseous. It lasted for only a short time, thankfully." Kathy also explained that she felt "pockets of icy cold air from time to time."

During an evening when everyone but Kathy was upstairs asleep in their beds, the young woman "heard something push down on the contents of the kitchen garbage can." Perhaps having that little housekeeping matter out of the way, the ghost felt it was time to join Kathy and relax, for she next "heard the sound of someone sitting on one of [her] chesterfields."

Kathy Smith had an admirably positive attitude about her circumstances. Rather than fearing the invisible being with whom she seemed to be sharing her home, she simply acknowledged what was happening.

"On many occasions, things went missing in our house. We would look all over, but they would not be found until much later when we weren't looking for them. They were found in the place that we had left them and [where we'd] looked for them many times," she explained. Although Kathy admitted that this "became quite annoying after a while," she didn't view the pranks as malevolent. "It was definitely a ghost with a sense of humour."

The phantom was not always positive: "One day when my sister Lori was babysitting my daughter Jackie, Lori felt something grab her leg. She turned to see what, or who, had done it ... there was no one there. Later that same day, Lori sent Jackie to her room upstairs to get some training pants from her drawer. Suddenly, Jackie began to scream very loudly."

The child's aunt ran to the little girl. "When Lori reached her, she was standing in her room shaking, pale and wide-eyed. Jackie pointed to a corner in her room and said, 'Man! Man in my room!'" Lori could not see a man in the bedroom but, after her own experience of being clutched at by an invisible force, she presumed that the ghost had been there but "had made a hasty retreat."

That explanation might be correct, but it's also possible that, as an adult, Lori was simply not capable of seeing what little Jackie could sense. Children can often see presences that adults cannot.

Animals, too, are able to detect manifestations not apparent to the adult human eye. "Our two dogs, Sandy and Toby, were very sensitive to the comings and goings of our resident ghost. Little Toby, the Chihuahua, often stood at the bottom of the stairway leading upstairs and barked viciously at the top landing."

The dog was clearly reacting to something only he could see. "Both Sandy and Toby watched, on many occasions, an unseen being come down the stairs and move across the living room," Kathy recalled. "It was definitely a strange sight to observe."

It is perhaps not just coincidence that the one time Kathy actually saw the ghost, she was pregnant. During puberty, youngsters are often especially sensitive to, and even attractive to, paranormal entities. Pregnancy is also a time of hormonal upheaval, and Kathy's pregnancy may have been a contributing factor in the encounter.

"I was several months pregnant with my second daughter and was getting up many times during the night to visit the bathroom. One such night, upon returning to bed, I saw him. He was standing near our bedroom closet. There was a large window behind him so all that was visible to me was his silhouette. I could see that it was a male, about 5'6" [1.7 metres] tall, with short hair and a medium build. I found it very strange that, although I had to walk within inches of the apparition, I felt no fear. I simply went back to bed and slept until morning."

Even though she did not fear the supernatural manifestation, Kathy consulted her next-door neighbour and friend who was "involved in the study of the supernatural." The neighbour "volunteered to speak to our ghost and help him move on if he was stuck where he was. She spent about fifteen minutes alone at my place while Jackie and I were at her house, waiting for her return. When we went back to my house, I could not believe what I smelled. All over the house there was a fresh aroma of mint in the air. I did some research of my own and discovered that when a house is 'cleared' of spirits, the smell of fresh mint is left behind."

Kathy concluded, "There were never any more unnatural occurrences in our home." Although that was the result Kathy had hoped for, she acknowledged "in some ways I miss the ol' guy."

She didn't know it at the time, but Kathy did not have long to wait before another supernatural presence found her.

"Since we moved away from Edmonton [to a small town slightly north and west of the city], we figured we would be safe from any more ghost encounters, especially since we bought a new home. Trouble is, we bought a place directly across the road from a very old cemetery.

Kathy further explained, "The first hint that something was amiss in our new home came when a book kept falling into the toilet. It was far enough away that it could not have been knocked in by one of our cats. It would have had to travel 3 feet (1 metre) to get to its destination. The events stopped happening when my husband stated emphatically, 'We are not moving.'"

Gary's emotional outburst may have quelled the spirit with the penchant for wet books, but the Smith family was in for some considerably less pleasant surprises.

"Things were rather quiet until one of our dogs brought home a strange little leather bag tied with a leather thong." Kathy said that the unusual satchel contained some feathers and many other objects that, for the most part, the Smith family was not able to identify. As nothing about the carefully crafted container meant anything to anyone in the family, and was literally "something the dog had dragged in," Kathy explained that they simply "put it away on a shelf."

Unfortunately, that innocent act created serious repercussions for the young family. "Shortly after that, our luck turned bad. Our health, physical and financial, took a turn for the worse. The only one unaffected by illness was our older daughter Jackie. We lost animals in accidents and it just seemed we could do nothing right. About two years after the leather bag was put away, I was talking about it to a teacher at the school I was attending. His face turned a strange shade of white and his mouth dropped. I asked him what was wrong and all he would tell me was 'Get rid of the bag.' He wouldn't tell me what it was or why he was so upset. He told me to take it to an Elder at the reserve near our home and the Elder would know what to do with it. I did as he said and since then things have started to get better for us."

Although relieved, Kathy was still puzzled about the origins of the strange leather purse and its possible connection to the unhappy times the family had endured. "I found out later that the bag was an Indian medicine bag which was put on [a] grave .... I guess the [deceased] owner of the bag was upset that we had it and apparently was the source of our bad luck. I have since discovered that the person who put the bag on the grave is a neighbour and friend of ours."

Knowing all that did nothing to explain where the bag came from originally or whose spirit its presence in her home had disturbed. It is possible that the presence in the Smith home had come to seek revenge upon those who had the medicine bag that should have been on his or her grave.

Buying a house near a cemetery can be a grave undertaking.

Bad luck hasn't been the only "visitor" the family has had from that nearby cemetery. "One day while I was on the phone with a friend of mine, I looked up and saw a very large man in a fedora and a trench coat walk into my bedroom. My daughter was playing in her room and her door closed by itself. Another day I was walking out of the bathroom and the doorknob on the same door rattled back and forth and the door opened by itself. I could not find anything in her room that would have caused that to happen.

Many nights she would come out of her room and tell us that she could hear scratching noises and voices calling her name and talking to her. I took her to our doctor to see if he could help find out if it was a medical problem but he could find nothing wrong. Thankfully, it did pass."

During the summer of 2000 the family did some home improvements. Part of these endeavours involved mixing concrete. A friend named Tracy was helping with the process "when she matter-of-factly informed me that we were being watched." Kathy noted, "I was surprised. Our nearest neighbours are a half-mile away. [Tracy] said that she saw a slim blonde lady in a 1920s-style dress watching us from the driveway. Tracy said that the woman looked rather perplexed as she watched Tracy shovelling gravel into the mixer. I can just imagine that women may not have done such work back when [the ghost] was alive."

The incident soon became even more dramatic. "I spoke with my stepfather about the apparition and he thought for a moment and then described her perfectly, even though I told him nothing specific about her. He is quite psychic."

If the most important single quality about a real-estate investment is "location, location, location" then it would seem that this house, with its proximity to a cemetery, had it all. Thankfully these particular homeowners accept their ethereal visitors and have continued to live in their house with the unique location, a house that is sometimes haunted, and sometimes not!

Protective Presence

We generally think of a haunted house as one having a resident ghost. The house Jim Lawrence described to me seemed to have acquired, if not a ghost, then a personality—a wise, protective and caring personality. In a letter to me, Jim relayed the story of this very special home with eerie simplicity.

Jim explained that in June 1969 he and his wife purchased a 100-acre (40-hectare) farm in Quebec's Eastern Townships about 100 miles (about 170 kilometres) east of Montreal and just north of the Vermont border.

The house on the property was a century old and, according to Jim, "in very poor condition." He explained that the place was "heated with an oil burner in the living room and a wood stove in the kitchen. Cold water was available to the kitchen [but] we needed to go outside to an outhouse."

Even the most optimistic real-estate agent would conclude that these conditions went well past "rustic," so the Lawrences embarked on some changes. "In October of that year, we had our first child. Every weekend, we would make the trek from Montreal, where I worked in the advertising business, to our little farm at the base of Owl's Head Mountain" to work on the property.

Jim continued, "Renovations were slowly taking shape when winter arrived. One very snowy December Saturday, the temperature dropped to about −40° F [at that point, by coincidence, the Centigrade and Fahrenheit scales meet]. We were working inside and cranked the oil burner up as far as it would go and stuffed the wood stove with hardwood logs."

Despite these extra attempts to keep the place heated, Jim reported that "gradually we noticed it was getting colder and colder inside the house. The burner and the stove weren't keeping the cold out at all. I tried [to turn on] the water at the sink [but] it was frozen."

The couple began to worry. After all, they weren't responsible for just themselves any more. The well-being of Catherine, their infant daughter, also rested with them.

"We discussed how cold it was getting inside the house and I checked the wood stove to see if it was still burning. I put my hand on the top of the stove and it was barely warm, although the fire was roaring in the firebox. Likewise, the oil burner was not putting out any heat, although I could see the fire in the pot was burning strongly."

The two main rooms of the house should have been considerably warmer than they were, but Jim and Eve were concerned about not only the lack of heat but the strange circumstances as well. They decided to stop their work and immediately drive back to Montreal.

When Eve lifted the baby out of her crib to carry her to the car, the young mother was shocked to find "the child was burning with fever." The woman took the baby's temperature, and sure enough, it was dangerously high—103° F (39° C).

Realizing they faced a potentially life-threatening problem, the Lawrences bundled their child in blankets and prepared to leave. Strangely, once these last-minute preparations were under way, "all of a sudden the wood stove and the oil burner began to put [out] heat."

The change was so dramatic that the worried father had to take time to "damper them down." One final precaution against the house being damaged in their absence was equally puzzling. "I decided to leave the tap running in the kitchen and turned it on again ... the water was running freely."

Not daring to take the time then to investigate this sudden reversal in the home's temperature, the couple drove toward medical help as quickly as the road conditions allowed. "On doctor's advice, we had to rub [the feverish infant] down with alcohol and then bathe her in a bathtub of ice and water to get the temperature down."

Jim Lawrence concluded his account of that phenomenal Saturday so many years ago by writing, "To this day, my wife and I believe the house (into which we moved full-time and lived in for the next twenty-five years) forced us to leave because the baby was sick. Had we not returned to Montreal when we did she would have died."

Had the old farmhouse become haunted or had it somehow become imbued with human qualities? We can never know for sure, but we do know that a series of bizarre coincidences was somehow set in motion, a chain of events created by an unseen enigma, which saved a baby's life.

This ghost or possibly a different one haunted the "very old barn" near that house. "I started a hobby farm," Jim began, before adding parenthetically "which turned into not a hobby at all—I milked thirty-five head of Holsteins in later years." Jim explained, "I kept calf feed and cow grain in different steel barrels. I had only one plastic scoop that I kept in the barrels. The scoop was never where I'd put it when I came in [to the barn] to do morning chores. It would be on the tractor seat, or on the floor, or on a window shelf or up in the hay mow. One morning I found the grain out of the barrels up in the hay mow and the barrels filled with a bale of hay each. These things happened even when there was freshly fallen snow outside and no prints in the snow."

Playing little tricks on the living seems to be standard ghostly fare and, for years, Jim and his family shared their heritage property with a phantom prankster who may also have been responsible for alerting them to their daughter's illness.

Island Entities

Prince Edward Island may not have a large population of flesh-and-blood citizens, but it certainly has a good-sized collection of ghostly legends! The following sad story about a haunted house in Abrams Village, on the west coast of the Island, came to me via Ontario. It highlights how very cruel humans can be to each other. In this case, the simple torment that a wife wrought upon her disabled husband was so cutting that, many years later, its effects remained embedded in the very atmosphere of the house in which they'd lived.

It is difficult to tell what era the ghosts were from because the house was thought to be nearly two centuries old. The following incident occurred in the 1980s, when a couple lived in the house.

One evening as the husband sat in the living room relaxing, his wife was in the kitchen making a pot of coffee for the two of them. When the brew was ready, she carried two steaming mugs out into the living room, setting one down on a table near her husband. The man thanked his wife for the drink, took a sip and set the mug back down on the table.

The husband soon reached for his cup again. But the cup wasn't where he'd put it down only a moment before. Instead, it was on the other side of the table.

Thinking his wife was playing a silly prank, he simply reached for the mug, drank from it and put it back beside him on the table. Moments later, the scene replayed itself.

Wondering what he was up against—a wife in a playful mood, or something even more puzzling—the man turned his full attention to the coffee cup. Seconds later, he watched in amazement as his cup moved away from him. His wife was certainly not involved because she had not moved. Only the cup had moved and it was once again out of his easy reach.

Later, after making discreet inquiries and being especially attentive to stories that the older folks in the community told, the couple understood what had happened in their home that evening. It seemed that an elderly couple had, at one time, lived in the old house. The husband had become crippled with arthritis, making even small movements very painful for him. One pleasure he still enjoyed, though, was an after-dinner cup of coffee. His cruel wife would torment him by setting his mug down at a spot on the table just out of his reach.

It was the ghostly echo of that cruelty that the owners in the 1980s had witnessed.

Ghostly Helper

This story from Prince Edward Island is about a decidedly kind ghost. A miller lived in Queens County, in the southwest of the Island. He was well liked within the community because he was honest, friendly and turned out high-quality flour. The story begins when he and his family became ill and were confined to their beds. The mill, their only source of revenue, stood still and silent in the yard adjacent to their home. There was grain to be milled, but the miller was too ill to attend to it.

One night, the miller and his family were awakened by the sound of the machinery working in the mill. Sure that intruders had broken in, the man gathered all his strength about him and, arming himself with as large a stick as he could find, headed out to investigate.

He cracked open the mill door. Inside, all the presses were working smoothly yet the place was completely dark. Over the noise of the running equipment he could hear footsteps but, at first, he couldn't see anyone inside. Moments later, his eyes having adjusted to his dark surroundings, he saw the shape of a man. Too surprised to speak or even move, the miller watched this mysterious image as it went about operating the mill in a way so familiar to its owner.

When he was able to collect his wits, the miller called to the presence. The sound of the human voice put a sudden end to all the activity. Even more puzzled now, the miller lit as many lanterns as he was able to from his spot near the only door into the building. He could see no one.

No one passed him to leave the mill and yet, there, not far from where he stood, were three bags of milled grain. A phantom had come, during the night, to help the ill and near-destitute family.

"Funky" Haunted Apartment

April now lives in Calgary, but she clearly remembers her years as a student attending university in Brandon, Manitoba. Her academic and social life may well have been remarkable, but it was her home life—in a haunted apartment—that she chose to tell me about.

"I got myself a very funky, single woman, attic apartment," April explained. "I'd been living there only two or three nights. I was sitting on the couch and all of a sudden I remember becoming incredibly terrified. Petrified. I couldn't stay in the room. I couldn't stay in the apartment. I left and went out. I walked the streets for a few hours that night and made up my mind that I was going to come back to confront whatever it was in my apartment that was terrifying me."

The young woman summoned her courage. ("I was nineteen and cocky then," she explained.) "I came home and spoke out loud to whatever it was in my living room. I said, 'Look, I don't know who or what you are but I'm living here now and we have to share the place, so get used to it.'"

April's impromptu exorcism was, it seems, effective because she wrote, "I never got bothered after that."

Apparently, though, the ghost was still in residence. "A couple of years later a friend was staying over at my place. It was in the winter. It was very dark out, 5:00 or 6:00 in the evening. He had fallen asleep on the couch. He heard something and thought it was me. It wasn't. He saw a woman pass through the hallway and he called out. He felt absolutely terrified but he didn't know why. He went down the hallway toward the bedroom and there was nobody there."

A while later April came home. "He told me the story. I just laughed and said, 'Oh, she's back.'"

Despite her apparent complacency, April was a little curious. "I have another friend who came [to visit and who] claimed to be psychic and sat down in the living room and said that there had been an unhappy woman there who had committed suicide many years before."

Such confirmation didn't surprise April as "one other friend had also seen her and been quite terrified."

That April had not mentioned the possibility of a ghost in her apartment to anyone makes her friends' reactions even more interesting.

Despite sharing her apartment with a ghost, April made a success of her academic career. She even reflects positively about the occasional fright that the spirit gave her and her friends. "I was there for five years. It was quite interesting. I've never had anything like that happen since."

With some ghost stories there can be a question as to whether it is the place or the person that is haunted. In this case though, it's evident that ghost was associated not with April but with her "funky" apartment in Brandon.

Suburban Spirits

Diane began her letter to me about her experiences living in a haunted house with the rhetorical question, "Where to start?" By the time I finished reading her note, I could understand her quandary. She certainly had ghost stories to tell.

Roughly seven years ago, Diane and her family moved to a house on an acreage east of Edmonton. Diane wrote that shortly after they settled in, "one of my friends gave me a gift of some little plastic horses, which I lined up on a shelf. I'd come home after school periodically to find them moved or rearranged or even, occasionally, missing altogether."

In typical sibling style, Diane accused her older sister of having been in her room and moving the ornaments around. The older girl denied these accusations. When the strange activity kept up, Diane discussed it with a trusted friend. "My best friend Danielle jokingly suggested maybe I had a ghost," Diane recalled. "That piqued my curiosity and we dragged out the good old Ouija board."

Diane and Danielle were in for an informative time of it. "We learned that there was the ghost of an eight-year-old girl in my room. She said her name was Kaytie." Suspicious that somehow her friend had manipulated the board's pointer, Diane felt that a second experiment was required. "I brought in two more of my friends," Diane continued, before explaining that these particular friends were carefully chosen for their lack of knowledge about the strange goings-on with the model horses.

"When Dave and Angele ... got on the board, they said someone named Kaytie had answered them. I was pretty

With a Ouija board, the medium has the message.

sure it was the same spirit because Dave remarked on how she spelled her name."

This second trial was enough to convince Diane that she did, indeed, share her bedroom with the ghost of a little girl. Fortunately, the natural and supernatural roommates seem to have accepted one another very well.

"I've gotten used to Kaytie's presence now, though sometimes she can be a little trickster. She loves re-arranging my porcelain figures and even, on occasion, my posters. (That impresses me; I have a lot of posters. Moving them is no mean feat.)"

While Diane is not alone, neither is Kaytie—on this plane or in her own ethereal realm—for there is a second presence in the house, one that Diane "discovered about three years ago." She explained, "I kept waking up to a cool touch on my face which, strangely, I never found frightening. At first, I thought it might be little Kaytie, lonely for company, which

isn't unusual but the more this occurred, the clearer my feelings on the presence were. This was an older, masculine presence, in his early to mid-twenties would be my guess."

This particular spirit has been a great comfort to Diane. "One night, I was sorely troubled by something that had happened that day, and the best I could manage was a fitful half-sleep in which my body was relaxed but my mind was ever active and alert. In that silence which comes only when the whole world is asleep, I clearly heard a soft, tenor voice, slightly accented, singing a soothing, Celtic-sounding melody. Of course, I opened my eyes searching for the source of the singing. In the darkness, I felt a cool breath on my face, clearly heard an exhalation, and a voice said softly, 'Sleep, lass.' That was the best sleep I'd had in months."

That second spirit identified himself as Gary. He informed Diane that he had died as a young man and was, therefore, forever twenty-three years old. Diane told me, "I've come to recognize the cool, soft scent in the air whenever he's around."

Were these spirits somehow associated with the house that Diane's family moved to or were they just wandering spirits attracted to Diane's warmth? Perhaps the spectres felt that Diane would be a companionable corporeal being and, in return for her acceptance of them and her hospitality, they tried to comfort the young woman when she needed it. It's clear from the tone of Diane's letter that the spirits that haunt her house chose well, for she obviously appreciates her extraordinary mates.

Haunted Park

During a winter evening in 1969, Officer Rick Holmes (a pseudonym) steered the Toronto police force motorcycle he'd been assigned off The Queensway, a main thoroughfare in downtown Toronto, and onto the darkened grounds of High Park. One of his responsibilities that night was to patrol the area. He rode slowly over the enormous park's roadway system and found nothing out of the ordinary.

From the moment he'd driven away from the station a few hours earlier, the city had seemed unusually quiet. Normally Holmes would welcome a bit of action to break up the hours but, as today was his last period of work before a stretch of days off, he didn't mind having a mellow, uneventful shift.

Once he'd finished the park patrol, Holmes turned his motorcycle back toward The Queensway. As he was passing Colborne Lodge, a preserved, original old home-cum-museum in High Park, he decided to park beside the stately residence and do the paperwork he'd have to hand in at the end of his shift. Steadying his notepad on his knee and using an overhead street light for illumination, Holmes began to re-read the notes he'd taken over the last few shifts in order to make sure that they were as complete as they needed to be.

As he worked, a movement in the darkened surroundings caught his eye. It seemed to have come from an upstairs window in the Lodge. The officer knew for certain that no one should be in the museum at that hour, so he craned his neck to gain a better sight line. Yes, he was sure

She lived there, she died there, she's still there.

that there was a woman standing at the window—a thin woman wearing a period costume of some sort. With a firm tap to the kickstand, Holmes balanced the motorbike and went to investigate. When he looked up again, the image was gone. Holmes went to the front door and tried to open it, but it was locked. He then checked the back door and the windows he could reach—all were secure.

He certainly was not going to break into and damage a heritage building just because he thought he'd seen a figure at a window. Perplexed, but satisfied that no intruder could have broken into Colborne Lodge, the policeman decided that the image at the window was a figment of his imagination. He turned on the motorcycle and headed back out to finish his shift on the main streets south of Bloor Street.

The next day, Constable Holmes was not able to erase from his mind the image of what he was sure he had seen

the night before—the distinct figure of a woman standing at a second-storey window in a building that was locked and should have been empty. And so, even though it was his day off, Holmes decided to go back to the Lodge. This time, it would be open to the public and populated with staff. Although he was feeling pretty unsure about the place, he still needed some additional information if he was ever going to ease his mind.

The facts he heard from the helpful and informative staff at John and Jemina Howard's former home, Colborne Lodge, did nothing to convince the young officer that he had imagined anything the evening before.

Holmes was told that construction began on the "Regency-styled cottage" in 1836. By the time it was completed in 1837, the residence was truly the talk of the town. The building itself was a splendid, large, two-storey affair, surrounded by over 100 acres (40 hectares) of prime real estate atop a Toronto hillside, overlooking Lake Ontario. But those qualities were not what had tongues wagging; it was that the place had an indoor toilet—one of the first in the city.

At the time, "bathrooms" were usually located some distance from the house, owing to discretion and prevailing technology. It was a time when polite company did not even acknowledge that bodily functions existed; therefore, this modern convenience required some ingenuity to hide it. So that no guest would ever be offended by seeing the entrance to the room that held this new-fangled contraption, the door to the bathroom was covered with wallpaper, camouflaged to blend in and look like a section of wall.

Obviously John Howard was one of the wealthiest men in Toronto at that time. He was an architect who also served

as the city's first engineer. Later in his life, Howard willed his huge estate and the buildings on it, including Colborne Lodge with its innovative flush toilet, to the citizens of Toronto for their use as a public park. Even today, High Park is one of the most beautiful inner-city parks in North America. The home is open to the visiting public as a period museum of sorts.

On the day that Rick Holmes returned to visit the old residence, a historical interpreter gave him a tour of the grand old place. Slowly, and hesitantly, he told her about his experience the night before. She showed little reaction to his story but did point out a framed portrait on the wall and told Holmes that it was the likeness of Jemina Howard, who had died a painful death in 1877—in the bedroom where Holmes had seen the apparition of a woman.

The man's reaction to the portrait was instantaneous. "That's who I saw," the startled policeman exclaimed. Although Holmes now had the answer to the question he'd come inquiring about, he likely left with even more questions—about the nature of life, death and the afterlife—than he'd had when he first walked into the house.

Holmes is not the only person to have detected Mrs. Howard's presence. Many visitors report sensing a female presence, which shouldn't be too surprising. All the ingredients are there for her ghost to be present. In life, Mrs. Howard was likely emotionally attached to her home. Her death took place there and her remains are buried in the immediate vicinity.

It would be difficult to imagine a more complete "recipe" for a haunting.

All in the Family

One beautiful morning in autumn 2000, Reta Laffin told me of the haunted house on the north shore of Nova Scotia where she has lived for most of her adult life. Much of what she told me related to the family of her late husband, Mac Laffin.

"The old farmhouse, well over a hundred years old, stands on a hill overlooking the Cobequid Bay. It is just a plain old house with no pretensions of grandeur," Mrs. Laffin began. "If it is indeed haunted, it is by friendly, ancestral ghosts. Mac's grandfather, Robert Laffin, was a seafaring man in his younger days." Reta explained that the sailor came to be honoured with the courtesy title of "Captain Bob."

She continued, "After Robert married Mary Cleveland, he gave up going to sea, got some land and settled in the house we are concerned with. He and Mary had a family of ten children, all born in the home."

The Laffin family believes that the house is "haunted by the ghost of Captain Bob, by the ghost of Mac's brother, Geo, and possibly by the ghost of Mac's mother."

"Geo was a veteran of the Second World War and returned with severe wounds, including the loss of his right hand. Geo also suffered almost total crippling of his left arm. He operated a small country store ... and lived a happy life. He died unexpectedly of a heart attack at the age of forty-one. He was asleep in his bed in the old home at the time."

"Strange and unexplained events have happened in this house over the years," said Reta.

The incidents described here all happened after Mac and Reta and their three children, Ellis, Dana and Patricia, moved into the house in 1961.

Shortly after moving into the old family home, the Laffins discovered some large family portraits, including one of Captain Bob, in the closet of what was known as the Five Islands bedroom. Reta explained, "The small room was called Five Islands because five islands were visible from the west-facing window. This was the room where Mac's great-aunt Clara had died young of galloping consumption or what's now known as tuberculosis."

When the family saw the portrait of Captain Bob, they all commented on the resemblance between their son Ellis and his great-grandfather.

"So close was this resemblance that it was almost uncanny. They had the same shape of face and features, both had mustaches but, most of all, both had pupils of their eyes of different sizes," Reta said. "For several months after the discovery of the pictures, every time family and friends visited, the Captain's picture was brought downstairs for all to admire and comment on the resemblance to Ellis. After the viewing, the picture was always returned to the closet along with the other pictures."

Initially, the family didn't make any connections between the portraits and what was to follow. Reta remembered that "several times, the family was wakened after midnight to the sound of thumping. The noise came from that room [the Five Islands bedroom where the pictures were stored]. Since no one was sleeping there we thought there might be a squirrel in the attic, or a rat in the wall, or branches might be hitting the roof in the wind. The thumping continued off and on, never on a regular basis, and always after midnight. Once, when it was particularly persistent, Mac journeyed down the hall. The only thing he noticed was that the closet door was open and Captain Bob's picture was facing the closet wall. He absentmindedly turned it to face out. The thumping ceased from that time on." Not surprisingly now "all of the Laffins are very careful to put the picture back facing outward after showing it off."

But those weren't the only ghostly disturbances in the Laffin home. Reta recalled when one of her future sons-in-law, Harold, was spending the night. "He was sleeping in the room directly across from Five Islands. As it was a very warm night, both bedrooms had doors left open for ventilation. Sometime during the night, the young man awakened. In the bright moonlight coming through the opposite window, he could see the silhouette of a man. At first, he thought he must be dreaming, so he sat upright to make sure he was awake. The figure stayed in full view for several seconds, then, all at once, it was gone. Harold thinks it was the same type of clothing that was in the portrait."

Harold wasn't the only future son-in-law to encounter a ghost in the Laffin home. One night the couple's older daughter, Dana, was entertaining her fiancé in the living room when suddenly they both heard footsteps in the upstairs hall. Reta acknowledged, "They both say that there seemed to be more than one set of footsteps and then the sounds became bolder and sounded as if they were going up and down the stairs. Neither one of them would investigate. Instead they went for a drive. Several hours later, they returned to a quiet house—no more footsteps."

Another evening when their parents were asleep, the sisters were watching TV in the living room. Reta told me that a dining-room window opened seemingly on its own. She described it as being "an old-fashioned window, the type that was always opened with great difficulty and needed a prop of some kind to hold it up. There was a good screen on the outside, so it couldn't have been opened from there."

Reta continued, "Not only did the window open, but it remained open with no visible means of support. The girls immediately set up a cry for mom to get up and get down there quick."

Of course, Reta ran to the children, "heard the girls' story, closed the window and admonished the ghost to stop this nonsense because the kids were frightened. Everyone thought this must have been [the ghost of] Geo."

But the sisters were not the only ones to be bothered by the ghosts. The Laffins' son also had an encounter. "Ellis tells of one time when he was alone in the house and he heard footsteps coming down the stairs and along the downstairs hall. The old-fashioned hall door was closed, held that way by an old-fashioned thumb latch. He heard the thumb latch rattle as if the door was opening. He immediately got up and looked, but there was no one in the hall." No one visible, that is.

Occasionally, over the years when Mr. and Mrs. Laffin were alone during an evening, they heard footsteps in the upstairs hall. Reta Laffin told me that they would "glance at each other, smile and keep on with their reading." If the steps continued for too long, one or other of them would call out "Go to bed Geo" and the footsteps would cease.

Mac, Reta's husband, died in his sleep early in the morning of October 2, 1994. Like his father before him, he died in the house he was born in. Reta recalls that on the first anniversary of Mac's death, she "had taken some ornaments off a shelf in the television room and packed them away in a box." Later in the day, she put a music box that had been a gift on her and Mac's fortieth wedding anniversary on the shelf.

Not long after, Reta heard a thud. At first, she thought she'd heard a car door slamming, but there was no car outside. The music box, however, was no longer on the shelf. It was "lying on the floor. On the rug next to a metal furnace register. It must have fallen from the shelf to the floor, but there was not a crack or chip on it." Reta picked it up and said, "Okay Mac, if you don't want it there, I'll put it back where it belonged."

Reta continued, "This year, on the sixth anniversary of Mac's death, I woke up in the night in the same room that he and Geo had died in. It's my bedroom now, you know, and I'm not squeamish. The hall light went on for no apparent reason. I thought maybe it was my son-in-law Harold but when I called he didn't answer. So I got up and went to the bathroom. On my way back from the bathroom to get ready to go downstairs, the light went out. He's still around here. We all believe that these are such friendly ghosts."

By way of an explanation for all the ghostly goings-on in her home, Reta Laffin points out that a "house that is more than a hundred years old has walls that have heard the secrets of several generations. There have been at least nineteen children born inside these old walls, at least six deaths and, in all likelihood, there are some that we do not know of. This old house has seen births, deaths, joy, sorrow, good times, bad times, laughter, tears, love, hate, passion, pain, all the various emotions of the Laffin generations have been inside these old walls. To the Laffins, [the spirits] are part of the family tradition ... welcome additions to our heritage." After all, how many families can claim resident ghosts?

Jumpin' Jammers

The Landrys are a family of musicians whose lives away from music have been repeatedly and profoundly affected by supernatural events. Bob Landry, the father of the group, began a recitation of his family's amazing encounters over the years with the assertion "these are a few stories involving the paranormal, or strange, stories we shall call them but they are true. They have been witnessed by several people. The first one [my son] Chris is going to tell us. It is about a house that the band had rented in Moncton. This was around 1976."

At that point Chris took over telling the story of the haunted house. "There was always a smell of sewer in the basement. Four or five times we had plumbers come in but they couldn't find anything wrong, several times the sewer would back up and [workers would] come in and fix it but they never could find a reason why it kept backing up."

Finding living and working accommodations for a band could not have been easy and so the group apparently decided not to be picky.

"My brother rented the house knowing this anyway and we started practising," Chris began. "One night we were practising and with a full band it gets pretty loud. It was snowing outside and we heard these three big bangs on the front door. We stopped and went to the door. Nobody was there [and there were] no footprints in the snow or anything. We thought maybe someone was around the back of the house playing tricks so we kept practising and we heard it again so we stopped [playing again]. We opened the door, there was nobody there again. The third time, we stopped, opened the door, [and again] nobody there. We were starting to get pretty upset. We took a break in another room and noticed that the record player was turning—backwards. It wasn't even turned on. It wasn't even plugged in!"

Chris and the other members of the band were never able to figure out what had caused the interruption to their practice session or the record player to turn backwards on its own. They didn't know it at the time but the house, or whatever force was at work in the house, had more surprises in store for the group.

Chris continued, "We went in one afternoon and nobody was in the house. We went up in the attic. There was a bed on the floor and it looked like somebody was lying in the bed. We called out the guy's name whose bed it was and there was no answer. We walked up to the bed. The blankets [looked as though] somebody was underneath them. When we got about 3 feet [1 metre] from the bed all the blankets just fell down fast."

The bed was empty.

Thoroughly frightened by what they had just witnessed, two of the young men with Chris decided to leave the house. As they headed down the stairs they passed a window "that could never be closed because it was painted [open], sealed in place," Chris explained.

Whatever force was at work confirmed the young men's decision to leave—as they passed it in their rush to flee from the haunted bedroom, the permanently opened window "slammed right down in front of them."

Chris acknowledged that the two who fled "never came back into that house." As a conclusion to this strange story of invisible forces, the man confirmed, "soon after, we moved out [too]."

Then, it was Bob Landry's turn to recall a supernatural incident in another house in New Brunswick—this in the town of Beersville, near Branch, north and west of Moncton.

"We had rented a house, myself and my three sons. We were going to compose some songs and get them ready for some shows we wanted to put on. The house was down in a valley, kind of isolated, a beautiful setting," the older man began. "We got there on the first night, just son Mark and I. We were sitting down on the sofa, talking about music and all of a sudden we hear like an army of rats running behind the walls."

"Good Lord!" the pair exclaimed before Mark noted, "That doesn't sound like normal rats. There can't be that many, we haven't seen any around."

Bob added ominously, "That was the first thing."

Once the strange sounds subsided, the father and son

tried to get on with their work. All their equipment, including a set of speakers that stood almost 2 metres (6½ feet) high, was set up in one large room in the house. The arrangement suited the musicians perfectly but apparently it wasn't to the liking of whatever presence was in the house with them.

"One night we were practising. There was a tuner on one of the speakers. Now a tuner, I would say, weighs about 2 pounds (just less than 1 kilogram) and all of a sudden, while we were playing, the tuner just flew right across the room. It was just as if somebody had picked it up and thrown it. Then we heard music coming from the record player in the other room but we had not turned it on. We went in there and there was a record playing—backwards."

From that moment on, none of the family of musicians questioned that they were in a haunted house. The proof of that theory was to continue.

"A few days later, we were all sleeping in the middle of the night and we heard this bang against the house. I thought a truck had driven off the highway and had come down in the valley but we went outside and there was nothing. I thought it might have been an animal too, but there were no tracks in the snow. We went into the kitchen where we had an old wood stove. The bang had been so hard that it had separated the stovepipe. The black soot was all over the floor from where the stovepipe had been separated." This physical evidence proved that what they had heard had been real.

"We thought there might be some kind of demonic possession so we had a priest friend come in and say mass.

After that we didn't have any problems." They did, however, have one further instance of supernatural intervention. "We had an artist friend of ours, Sid, who wanted to come stay with us and do some paintings because the scenery was so beautiful."

Bob explained, "The boys and I, we'd go in to the bedroom and shut the door and say the rosary. Sid was not a Catholic so we respected his privacy. One night he came out of his bedroom and said, 'If your Blessed Virgin is so powerful, why doesn't she send us some chicken?' We had been living on rice and beans and bologna so he said, 'Why doesn't she send us some chicken?' Well I said, 'We'll ask her. She might, but first we should be thankful for what we've got. Some people don't even have that.'" That night, the little group left the issue at that, but the next morning, a car came down their driveway. Bob explained, "We had no telephone. John Majewski, a violin maker who had made a violin for Mark, came into the house with two chickens. We started laughing. We asked John how come he'd brought us some chicken."

The visitor replied, "This morning about 5:00 I heard a voice in my room say 'John,' and I said, 'Yes, Lord,' because it could only be the Lord. He says, 'I want you to bring the Landrys some chicken.' I said, 'Okay Lord, but I don't know where they live.' The Lord said, 'I'll show you.'"

Bob added, "John went back to sleep and about 8:00 in the morning this [neighbour] came in to get a violin that John had fixed. He asked her if she knew where to find the Landry family."

John's customer said that she did know where the Landrys were living and added, "I was there the other day visiting them."

"Will you take me there?" John asked.

The customer must have agreed to take John, for less than an hour later the challenge from the agnostic artist was answered and the chickens were delivered.

Bob chuckled as he recalled, "Old Sid didn't want to be too humiliated. He didn't want to admit that the Blessed Mary had brought us some chicken so he said, 'Why didn't she bring us some vegetables too?' About ten minutes later this nun from the parish about 15 miles (24 kilometres) away, Sister Louise, came down the driveway with two big shopping bags full of carrots and turnips and potatoes and all kinds of vegetables. She'd just cleaned out her garden and she thought the Landrys could use this."

At that final gesture, the family's disbelieving guest could only mutter, "I give up, I give up. I won't criticize the Blessed Virgin anymore." Bob Landry added that he would never forget the doubter's final comment.

"He said, 'I'm sold, I'm sold.'"

Mr. Landry also remembered being a guest in another haunted house.

"I had a band that had been hired to play for two weeks at the Officers' Mess at the American Air Force Base in Gander, Labrador. I wanted to add an instrument so I found a trumpet player."

The musicians still needed to find a place to practise. The newest addition to the band, the trumpet player, volunteered his own home.

"It's nice and big," the man assured Bob, but Bob already knew something about the house this man and his wife lived in. "His house had the reputation of being haunted. It was an old sea captain's house around Hillsborough, New Brunswick, not far from the Bay of Fundy. I asked him, I said, 'Did you ever hear that this house is haunted?'"

The newcomer to the band acknowledged that Bob was right. There were ghosts in his house.

As with many houses in that area this one included a widow's walk where, Landry explained, "the wives of the seaman used to go to watch for their loved ones to come home," and the widow's walk was the centre of this particular haunting.

Bob recalled, "Apparently what was happening was the musician and his wife would walk out of the house at night with all the lights turned off. They would go out the driveway and look back. The light in the widow's walk was always on. Not only that but they couldn't sleep there at night. They had to work at nights because when they were home on weekends at night they heard footsteps coming up the stairs toward the widow's walk, the sound of a sobbing woman and a door close. Then they wouldn't hear her again." The couple lived like that until, "one night they decided to tape record her sobbing. The man took a tape recorder into the widow's walk room and turned it on. [After leaving the room] he put masking tape all around the edges of the door. That night they heard the same sounds. The next morning they took the masking tape off the door and turned on the tape recorder. On the tape was the sound of someone climbing the stairs and sobbing."

The trumpet player offered to play the tape for Bob

Landry. Unfortunately, despite the fact that the man had been very precise about where he'd left the tape recorder with the supernatural sounds on it, neither the machine nor the tape could ever be found again.

The trumpet player and his wife have discerned that whatever spirit they share their house with resides in the basement when it's not active. He explained to Bob that, over the years, they had tried to have the old earthen basement of the house finished. They never succeeded, though, for as soon as the workers approach a particular underground area, "they just don't want to go any closer. For some reason they just can't get past a certain barrier. It isn't a visible [barrier] but really works on their mind. The story goes that this old sea captain came home and surprised his wife with someone else .... He killed them both and killed himself. And that," Bob Landry concluded, "is the true story of the sobbing widow of Hillsborough."

Patty Cake

Several Canadian radio stations include a live phone-in show with me on Halloween. I appreciate these shows because they are fun to participate in and give me a chance to hear ghost stories from people all over the country, people I might not otherwise ever make contact with.

The following ghost story came to me exactly that way. During a phone-in segment on Halloween 1999, a woman told me of her eerie experiences in an Ottawa haunted house.

The caller, a new mother whom we shall call Judy, began by explaining, "We moved into our house about two years ago. I used to rock my baby daughter in a chair." As soon as I heard that a child was involved in the ghostly encounter, I was especially eager to hear the rest of the tale. Children are usually much more receptive to the presence of spirits than adults are. If Judy hadn't been aware of that fact, she was about to become so, for her simple maternal action, soothing her baby, would be the beginning of an ongoing paranormal involvement.

Judy explained that while she was rocking the baby, who was "not quite a year old" at the time, the little one "used to put her hands out and play patty cake."

Perhaps that might seem normal enough — a child playing a child's game—except that the little girl seemed to be playing patty cake with someone else, someone her mother could not see, or hear, or feel or smell. Judy readily acknowledged, "I used to think this was strange."

Strange it may have been, but it also must have prepared

Judy for what was to come. At the time Judy told me their story, her daughter was just under three years old and the ghostly games of patty cake had become a thing of the past.

That certainly didn't mean the ghost was no longer a part of their lives. The child's interaction with it had simply changed. "Now," says Judy of her daughter, "she talks to whoever's in her room."

Judy is still not able to see the presence, but she says it's obvious that her daughter does. "I know she sees something because I've seen her eyes follow [it] around the room. I would ask her [and] she would say it was an uncle or a grandpa. It's a man."

For the most part, the little girl and her invisible companion co-exist peacefully, but sometimes the spirit seems to annoy her. "She has a little table set in her bedroom and she gets quite angry when she's playing. I'll take this table set, and put it in another room, and she doesn't have any of the same actions that she does in her bedroom. That's why I'm sure that whatever it is, it's in her bedroom. I don't know if it's there to scare her, but at night she doesn't like it. It scares her then. She gets really scared."

The child was not the only one to become upset, Judy acknowledged. "It would freak me right out when she would follow [with her eyes] something moving around the room. She'd put her hands out to touch [it] and stand right up on my lap and look at something right behind me. I would turn my head to see what she was looking at and, of course, I wouldn't see anything. But I know she did."

Curious about the intruder that only one person in the family could see, Judy asked her daughter to describe it. When she asked her what it looked like, the girl made a "weird face. She scrunches up her mouth and it looks like an old man."

And, when Judy asks the little girl "Who are you talking to?" the child exclaims, "I don't know. I don't know."

To me, her emphatic disclaimer makes the story even more provocative. It would certainly be fascinating to learn who the spirit is, although in all likelihood even Judy will never know. Like most children, her daughter may simply grow out of her ability to see spirits and eventually forget that her former patty-cake pal ever existed.

Fred's Family Phantom

This story concerns some ghostly encounters experienced by the informant's cousin. I shall refer to my correspondent as Jan and her cousin as Beth. After you read about the following incidents and realize what happened to Beth, you will no doubt understand why the family does not want to be fully identified.

Beth's interactions with the supernatural began when she was a youngster living in her parents' home at Musselman's Lake, approximately 60 kilometres (37 miles) northeast of downtown Toronto. As do many young girls, Beth had an interest in the paranormal. Toward that end she purchased, and began to use, a Ouija board. Not long afterward, according to Jan, "peculiar happenings" began taking place in the house.

It seems that Beth's use of the Ouija board attracted a

spirit, first into her bedroom and then into the whole home. Jan stated, "Beth's first encounter with the spirit happened one night when she went to bed."

After all the years I've been collecting ghost stories, the one ghostly instance that still sends cold shivers down my back is any story that includes a component about a ghost getting into bed with someone. And that is exactly what happened to Beth. Jan wrote in her message to me that Beth "felt the weight of someone sitting on the side of her bed and immediately opened her eyes—but saw no one there."

Despite the lack of visual evidence, Beth was aware that someone had joined her in bed because "she felt a hand very gently stroke her face." Terrified, the girl shot out of her bed and ran downstairs to tell her father what had happened. The man was not only a skeptic but a strict father for, as Jan wrote, "He would not listen to her story of the invisible visitor and proceeded to brusquely lead her back to bed."

Apparently, the spirit did not like having its presence denied for, as Beth's father firmly escorted her back "up the stairs, a picture fell off the wall and crashed down in front of them. As if that wasn't enough of a sign, a piece of baseboard also came falling down from [a stair] above them."

The incident that night was only the beginning. "One evening, when Beth thought she was alone in the living room, she felt uneasy and sensed that she really was not alone. She looked over to the antique clock on the mantel and watched in disbelief as the hands of the clock spun around wildly."

By now, this family home was definitely a haunted

house. The sounds of phantom footsteps were becoming an everyday occurrence that even Beth's skeptical father, Fred, could not deny hearing. These disturbed the man on more than one occasion when he was working in his basement workshop. "He would come up to see who had come into the house and, of course, find no one."

Perhaps because he refused to believe in it, the entity seemed especially offended by Fred. "One morning, he came downstairs to breakfast and complained that his ribs hurt. He couldn't understand the shocked look on his family's face until he looked in the mirror. His face was covered with scratches." The man had no idea what happened to him through the night, although his family suspected that he was attacked by the ghost.

Another night, shortly after Fred had gone to bed for the night, "he heard a female voice tell him to go and check his truck. He ignored the request, dismissing it as his imagination, until a very emphatic order came from the same source, 'Go check your truck, NOW!'"

This order was difficult to refuse, so the man left his comfortable bed, went outside to where his truck was parked and discovered that his truck had been broken into and "some valuable property had been stolen."

Other family members began to get caught up with the ghost's antics. Beth's mother, Betty, was drying an antique plate that had been given to her by Fred's mother. Jan explained, "Betty had a firm grip on the plate but it flew out of her hand and broke into hundreds of pieces on the floor."

Other objects also began to move mysteriously. "A glass swan filled with old coins used to sit on a shelf in the kitchen. There were other knick-knacks in front of the swan but [just the swan] 'flew' off the shelf and hit the floor." Even the coins that had been in the swan remained on the shelf, along with the items that had been in front of the swan.

Not long after that incident, Beth and her brother, Chris, actually saw something of the house haunter. As Jan explained, "Chris made sure he was never alone in the house after he saw long, flowing, blonde hair stream up the stairway as he sat in the living room playing his guitar. Beth saw a shadowy figure stare down at her from the same stairway when she was alone." Chris's fiancée saw the spirit most clearly and described it as "a little blonde girl, about ten years old, dressed in Victorian-style clothes."

The most frightening sign of the spirit was also the most subtle: "Often the sound of a heartbeat could be heard throughout the house."

Other ghostly pranks were more commonplace—knocks would be heard at the front door, but there would be no one there, nor, in winter, would any tracks be visible in the snow. Objects hanging from a doorway would suddenly begin to twirl madly when no one was near them and there were no distinguishable drafts.

As with most families who live in a haunted house, this little group eventually accepted that yes, they had a ghost, but, no, she really wasn't harmful. At least, no more harmful than a living ten-year-old child.

In a fascinating postscript to the story, Fred died in the kitchen of that haunted house. As his children Beth and Chris were preparing to sell the place, they chose to paint the bathroom a colour that they knew their father would not like. They watched in awe as "the paint can suddenly floated out of the bathroom and deposited itself on the floor, exactly where Fred's body had been found."

Despite living in a haunted house, the man had remained a skeptic all his life but, in his afterlife, had become a ghost himself! Perhaps his spirit eventually befriended that of the little girl who had haunted his house for so long.

Twelve Stranded Men

Taloyoak (formerly Spence Bay) in Nunavat, Canada's newest territory, sits on a hillside at the southern end of the Boothia Peninsula, roughly 300 kilometres (186 miles) north of the Arctic Circle, and overlooking the frigid waters of the St. Roch Basin.

In November 1971, a team of twelve representatives from the territorial and federal governments was sent to Spence Bay on an information-gathering mission. Hours before the contingent was to fly out of this remote settlement, a severe arctic storm blew through the area, completely cutting the tiny village off from the rest of the world and stranding the civil servants in what was to them a very strange land.

While the storm raged across the barren stretch of snow and ice, the residents of Spence Bay shared their spartan accommodations with the marooned men. If any of those guests were not already terrified by the unfamiliar and potentially life-threatening situation they found themselves in, then being told ghost stories no doubt pushed them strongly in that direction. Worse, one of those ghost stories

Frozen in time

concerned the very residence in which they were to wait for the storm to abate.

According to a newspaper report in the *Edmonton Journal* on November 25, 1971, Ernie Lyall, who had lived in the North for most of his life, began by "casually" mentioning to the stranded visitors that the Hudson's Bay Company building they were sheltered in was haunted—haunted by the ghost of a murdered woman. The crime had taken place in winter some years before, just outside the community of Spence Bay. A timely burial was impossible as the ground was frozen. Lyall remembered that, instead, he and some others brought the corpse into the Hudson's Bay Company building where it lay until spring.

Evidence of the haunting began immediately after the funeral. "We were just starting to sit down to dinner one evening when the outer door opened and we heard footsteps coming into the room, then a person cleared her throat. We went to see who it was but there was nobody there," Lyall explained in a voice that carried over the howling gales blowing around and through the structure.

This pattern continued for many nights, Lyall told the men who were gathered in the building where the bizarre events had been witnessed. He recounted the time he hid under a desk for nearly half an hour in an effort to catch the prankster but did not see anyone. At that point, he gave up and went back to the table to finish his meal. He had no sooner sat down than he heard the door opening again. The sounds of these phantom knocks and footfalls went on "for the rest of the winter," the man acknowledged, and then added, "The people of this community say it is the spirit of the murdered woman ... and the ghost is said to still haunt the house."

Others of the visiting group gathered at another residence, the Spence Bay teacherage, where a sixty-six-year-old woman spoke to the government workers about a vicious fight that had taken place in the early 1900s between supernatural beings and a local shaman. In order to set the story, the woman first explained that, in those days, each family built and lived in an "ice house." A portion of the roof of each structure was formed by a clear block of ice, selected specifically to allow light from the outside into the living area. Each of the individual residences was linked to the dwelling on either side of it by way of a tunnel, thereby forming a chain of houses.

In the year the story took place, the community's shaman was experiencing terrible interference from the spirits of his predecessors. These deceased leaders and spiritual healers either did not approve of the way he was carrying out his

In ice houses such as this a shaman fought with ghosts.

responsibilities or, even in death, they were not willing to relinquish the important positions they had held.

One winter's day, as all the residents watched in fear, the shaman did physical battle with the ghosts of his forefathers. The fight went on for hours. Although the ghostly shamans were not visible to anyone but the living shaman, the woman relating the tale recalled that as the spirits moved from house to linked house, their shadows blocked out the light streaming in through the clear piece of ice in each roof.

The visitors listening to this story may, at first, have taken it to be a fanciful piece of folklore until the woman telling the tale acknowledged that she had been a witness to the struggle and that the shaman had come away from the altercation suffering from deep knife wounds on his arms and scalp.

Even the most skeptical southerners had a difficult time discounting such graphic evidence of the otherworldly altercation.

Haunted Honeymoon

When Margarette Atkinson penned the story of the first weeks of her marriage, she titled it "My Spirited Island Honeymoon." The adventure began with her wedding on Valentine's Day 1941. Like most young men during those years of the Second World War, the groom was an enlisted man. He was training in the British Columbia town of Nanaimo, on Vancouver Island, so both the bride and groom considered it lucky that he had managed to find a tiny, two-room cabin about 5 kilometres (3 miles) from the base for them to live in.

A few days after the wedding, the groom returned to his military duties. Margarette stayed behind, alone, she thought, in the isolated cottage, "to keep house." Her experiences soon indicated that she had company—of a ghostly nature. Fortunately, Margarette was blessed with an positive attitude and reported that she quickly settled into a pleasant daily routine "with Mr. & Mrs. Mouse, who had five little ones."

The evenings, however, were another matter. Often when she was alone, Margarette would be startled by noises outside the isolated honeymoon suite. Without fail, she would summon her courage, go to the door and check outside the cabin. Not finding any reasonable explanation for the sounds, the puzzled woman would retreat to the shelter of the cottage. Little did she suspect that these disturbances, and those that followed, were rudimentary attempts at communication—attempts by the restless spirit that haunted the tiny, isolated residence. The ghost's next efforts were clearer.

"Every night, after I lit the kerosene lamps, the enamelled doorknobs would turn back and forth. I'd slip out the back door and peek around the corner, but not a thing was out there," the woman recalled nearly sixty years later.

During her husband's first leave from his duties, Margarette learned that the strange phenomenon she was a witness to had definitely not been a figment of her imagination. "It went on every night. He'd watch it too."

In May, Margarette's husband was posted to Ontario. Before the couple left the Nanaimo area, they gave their forwarding address to a surveyor who was measuring the land around what Margarette called "my little haunted cabin." A month later, their foresight was rewarded and the reason their honeymoon cabin had been haunted became clear to them. "They found a perfectly preserved dead male, buried [on the lot]."

Today, reflecting on her first home, Margarette still views the time as a positive one—both for those living in the tiny house and the spirit that haunted it. "I felt safe. That spirit must have been glad of my presence, poor soul [he was] so all alone [and] I didn't know how to communicate [with him]."

Most of us have fond memories of our honeymoons, but not many of them include a ghost story.

Murdered Manifestation

Tadoussac, Quebec, is on the north shore of the St. Lawrence River where it meets the Saguenay River. Time's passage has allowed today's residents, for the most part, to remember only the pleasant aspects of their community's past. But at least one citizen is reminded daily that the "good old days" were sometimes brutal and unjust. A man we'll call Peter understands this fact because he owns and lives in a haunted house.

Although he's fond of his home, he knows it's not entirely his and that experiencing certain unpleasant sensations are part of the price he pays for living there. One room, directly above the kitchen, is home to the spirit of a maid who worked there in the early 1900s. For reasons that have been shrouded by the mists of time, the employer murdered the young woman. Her presence is still easily detectable in the room that was once "hers" and where, it is guessed, the murder took place.

Many people other than the current homeowner have reported being visited by the wronged entity. She manifests as a feeling (to the living) that they are not alone, which is not surprising, of course, because they are not—she, the spirit of the ghostly maid, is always within those particular four walls.

One guest who was invited to tour the home said "Cold chills ran through me. I had to leave the room. I was not welcome there."

We can only hope that the poor young soul will finally go to her eternal rest and that the homeowner's companions are now only of the flesh-and-blood variety.

Old House Haunter

The woman who told me about this New Brunswick haunted house has been a friend of mine for many years. We were next-door neighbours in a suburban Toronto townhouse development when all of our children were small. Since then, Joanne has moved east, I have moved west, our children have grown and we are both grandmothers. Throughout this time, we have remained at least sporadically in touch, and I have always remembered a passing comment Joanne made in a letter she wrote to me not long after she, her husband and his children, had settled into their big old home in Hopewell Cape, New Brunswick. Joanne said she thought the house was haunted. Even though I was not writing books of ghost stories at that time, I have always been fascinated by them, and so, of course, her comment stuck in my mind.

When I began to write this book, my old friend's words came back to me. I sent her a message asking for details of the haunting and for permission to use her story. Her positive and complete reply came via e-mail within twenty-four hours.

My former neighbour sent photographs of the house so I know it was painted white and was a very big, old place. It looked like the kind of house I always hope will have a resident ghost. For the sake of family serenity, Joanne probably didn't harbour similar hopes, nor, for the first few days, did she even suspect that the place was haunted. Nevertheless, it didn't take long before she suspected and later knew for sure she was sharing her home with someone or something that had been there for a very long time.

My friend began her story simply. "Yes," Joanne confirmed, "I do believe we had a ghost in our house in Hopewell Cape."

Although she no longer lives in the house, it is more than likely still home to the ghost, who Joanne believes may have been one of the original residents. "The house is quite old and was built by a sea captain, Captain Hoar, I believe. It has a widow's walk on the roof of the house and you could get up there by ladder. At one time, there was a set of stairs going up there, but one family moved the stairs to the basement, as the wife was pregnant and needed the stairs to go down to tend the fire. When I first moved in, Doug [my husband] was on the road a lot."

Having set the stage for describing her experience, Joanne continued explaining an event that occurred just one week after they moved into the house. "I remember very clearly what happened. I had stripped all the wallpaper and repainted the bedroom. [Step-daughter] Jenny was sleeping across the hall. I was lying in bed and the room had a ceiling light with an old-fashioned shade that hung from three chains. I had been reading and had the ceiling light on. When I got tired, I turned off the light and switched on the bedside lamp. I was not even dozing when I heard a scratching sound. It was coming from the ceiling shade, almost overhead [but] more to the foot of the bed."

Joanne knew something out of the ordinary was going on. She "watched in fascination as the chains, two of them, loosened and lifted off the hooks they were attached to. The shade started swinging, suspended by the remaining chain."

Who or what caused the light fixture to swing?

"There was nothing on the ceiling that could have caused it to loosen the chains" and therefore account for these very deliberate, controlled and effective motions. Nothing Joanne could see, hear, or smell, that is.

Never having had any previous experience with the supernatural, Joanne was, in a word, terrified. At the same time, though, she was fully aware that she had a little girl to be responsible for.

"I didn't want to scream and scare Jenny, so I lay there, paralyzed. I watched as it [the light] swung for a while then slowed down to a stop. I decided right there and then to make friends with whatever spirit was playing with me. I don't think I talked out loud, but made some sort of mental agreement that I would give him/her the space they needed."

This consideration is very much in character with Joanne's pragmatic approach to life.

"The next morning, I reattached the chains and they never came down again," my friend explained.

After that incident, Joanne was convinced that she could never be entirely alone in her "new" house. Subtle inquiries around the community confirmed her presumptions. "Neighbours have told me since that the house had ghosts, [although] I never got any concrete stories from them."

The closest Joanne ever came to hearing of anyone else's encounter with the phantom came in the form of a vehement denial.

"One night, I had a grandmother and her granddaughter stay at the house. The grandmother had lived in the house years before. I found it amazing that so many people would come back to visit the house. Well, I asked her if she had any encounters. 'NO!!' she said very abruptly."

Joanne "was taken aback" by the sudden difference in the older woman's tone and attitude. "She was so sweet and all of a sudden she got this look on her face. I just know there was a story there, but I guess I'll never know."

And, sadly, neither can we. We can only hope that the ghost's current houseguests are as thoughtful and sensitive about its presence as Joanne was.

Musical Manifestation

When the Robbins family moved into the old house near St. James Anglican Cemetery, they were fully aware that they were buying a piece of Winnipeg's history. Their "new" home had been the residence for one of the first Anglican bishops assigned to serve the community. Looking forward to living in this bit of Canadian heritage, Mr. and Mrs. Robbins, along with their two teenage sons, Jay and Alan, settled in easily.

Both Jay and Alan had dreams of becoming famous rock musicians. Alan, the older of the two, faithfully practised guitar, and Jay decided to learn to play keyboard instruments. With money saved from a part-time job, the aspiring musician purchased an electronic organ and put it in the basement.

One day, as Mrs. Robbins was preparing dinner in the kitchen on the main floor, Jay went downstairs to plunk away at the keyboard, practising his scales and trying out the sheet music for some very simply constructed tunes. At that very moment, Alan was in the bedroom the boys shared, on the second floor of the house, fooling around with his own new interest—automatic writing. Alan had heard about the phenomenon from some of his classmates and was eager to try his hand at it.

The procedure seemed easy. Apparently, all one had to do was sit comfortably with a pen poised above a sheet of paper and wait for some mysterious force (a spirit, the kids at school suggested) to begin to work through the writer's hand by moving it in such a way as to form letters, then words and, ultimately, a message "from beyond."

Although he sat at his desk and waited patiently for nearly half an hour, his arm resting on a pad of paper, his hand loosely holding a sharpened pencil, not so much as a mark showed up on the page. Alan was disappointed but decided to try again later.

As Alan was putting away the evidence of his unsuccessful attempt to dabble in the occult, he heard some commotion downstairs. It sounded as though his mother and Jay were having a disagreement. He went down to the main floor to investigate, but Alan could see that his mother was no longer in the kitchen. From there, he could hear both his mother's and brother's voices coming from the basement. He could also hear music—beautiful, complex organ music. He went down to the basement.

Alan Robbins will never forget what he saw when he reached the bottom of the steps. Jay sat playing his new and largely unmastered electronic organ. Mrs. Robbins stood behind the boy, her hands on his shoulders exerting pressure to get him to back his body away from the instrument. In an increasingly stressed-sounding voice, she was ordering her son to stop playing, to stand up, to come upstairs with her and eat dinner.

For a long time, Jay seemed completely unaware of his mother's presence, let alone her entreaties. He played on, as though possessed by the melodic and dramatic music that was somehow emanating from his fingertips. Cautiously, Alan approached his brother. He could see that his brother had a rather odd look about him. The boy's eyes were glazed; Jay appeared to be in a trance of some sort.

Mrs. Robbins and Alan were far too concerned about Jay and what was happening to appreciate the complexity

An electronic organ played music from beyond.

and great beauty of the music "he" was playing. Eventually, Jay came to the end of the particular musical composition he'd been "playing" or, more correctly, as it turns out, "channelling." He sat still in front of the simple electronic organ that had been making sounds one would associate with a carefully modulated and skillfully played pipe organ. Slowly, the glazed look left his eyes.

For a time, all three members of the family remained quiet. Finally, Mrs. Robbins broke the silence with the simple statement, "Dinner's ready, boys."

Alan, Jay and Mrs. Robbins made their way up into the kitchen. There was little said through dinner—nothing about the extraordinary event that had just taken place. And, from that day on, neither the incident nor anything even remotely like it ever occurred again in the Robbinses' old house by the cemetery—the house that was once the bishop's residence. Jay and Mrs. Robbins never had any idea what had caused that single, supernatural, musical event in their home.

Alan never again fooled around with automatic writing or anything else of a paranormal nature for, to this day, he's convinced that his attempt to summon a spirit was successful. It just didn't manifest as words on a paper the way he had expected it would. The spirit he had conjured was obviously more interested in music than in writing. That simple but profound variation in his experiment's result taught Alan, once and for all, to respect the potential power and unpredictability of the spirit world.

Welcome Home

Anne and Nick were both in their thirties when they bought a haunted house in Kamloops, British Columbia. Anne explained that the house was "exactly what we were looking for. It met every requirement I'd set out to find. It was in our price range, just the right size and was in very good repair. Even the location met all my criteria; on the north shore, close to the river. It wasn't on a main through street so the children would be safe, even, in years to come, as they walked to school." The children Anne referred to were Chris, their three-year-old son, and a newborn daughter, Kate.

In retrospect, Anne realizes that she has commented many times to friends and relatives that the house was so perfect for them and that everything to do with the move went so smoothly that she wondered if the house hadn't chosen them, rather than the other way around.

Both children and their parents happily settled into their new place. With Kate's birth, they had really outgrown the place they'd just moved from, and Anne had been finding it harder to keep the small place tidy. "I'm something of a neat freak," she acknowledged with a chuckle. "I like the house to be orderly and the old house was just too small to be kept that way. It was feeling cluttered and I hated that."

After moving into the larger house, Anne began a morning routine that she and the children grew to love. "Before breakfast I used to bundle both kids up, put them in the stroller and go for an hour-long walk. I loved starting my day that way. Those walks remain happy memories for me. One walk, in particular, though, stands out in my mind."

Anne continued, "I'd been talking with a close friend, Joan, the day before. The subject of reincarnation had come up in the conversation. I told Joan that the idea of reincarnation appealed to me but that I wasn't sure I was entirely sold on the reality of the concept. Our talk was still on my mind the next day when I set out for my walk with the children."

That morning Anne had been up for over an hour before the children woke up. She'd enjoyed the peace and quiet by straightening a few things in the living room. "I put the baby swing exactly where I knew I was going to need it when I came home and shoved the ottoman up against the couch. The kids' toy box was in its corner and the two little kid-sized plush chairs were set at a specific angle."

Once the children woke up, Anne readied them for the day and then carried them both out the back door where the stroller stood. "We walked our usual route and enjoyed it as much as always. I realized then, though, that I'd be calling Joan later that day because I still couldn't get the topic of reincarnation out of my mind."

As she strolled along an idea came to Anne and she asked Chris, who was three years old at the time, "Do you remember before you were born?"

"Oh, yes," the child replied. "That's when I was old but I was still Chris and you were little." That innocent comment caused Anne to reflect further, but she put the idea aside as it was time to get home for breakfast.

"I unlocked the back door and let Chris into the house ahead of me. I picked Kate up and carried her into the house. My plan was to put her in the baby swing while I put some breakfast out for Chris. This wasn't something I gave much conscious thought to—not until I went to put Kate into her swing and found that it wasn't where I'd left it. I could hardly believe my eyes. I'd only left the house an hour before. I'd locked it when I'd left and unlocked it when I returned but everything in the living room that could be moved, had been moved."

Holding the baby and assuring Chris that she'd see to his breakfast right away, Anne stood in her own living room and stared. "Everything but the couch and the big chair had been pushed up against the front wall. I was shocked, to say the least."

Anne moved all the pieces of furniture back to where they belonged and where they had been an hour before. She then continued on her busy morning with the children as best as possible. As soon as she had the opportunity, she called her friend Joan. The two puzzled over Chris's comments and the disarray in the living room but, of course, could come to no conclusion.

"Are you going to tell Nick what happened?" Joan asked. "Not a chance," Anne remembers replying. "It would freak him out way too much."

After that, all was quiet in the family's home for nearly a year.

"It was Nick who encountered something next," Anne explained. "He kept smelling cigarette smoke in the house. It was driving him crazy because we don't smoke, nor do our next-door neighbours. Even the woman we bought the house from was a non-smoker. The smell of smoke wasn't constant. It would come and go but every time Nick smelled it he'd stop what he was doing and search the entire house. Several weeks later he happened to be chatting with a neighbour from the next block. The man had lived in the area for most of his adult life. He told Nick that the man who'd owned our house for years, and whose widow had sold it to us, had been not only a heavy smoker but also quite the practical joker."

When Anne heard that story she decided to break her silence about the strange events during that morning walk. The two events seemed to fit together and even reinforce Anne's sense that, when they bought it, the house had chosen them as much as they'd chosen it.

Since that time, Nick has occasionally smelled cigarette smoke in the house but he no longer worries about it. He just smiles at the thought that his young family is being watched over by a benevolent, cigarette-smoking, practical joker of a spirit.

And, as for the ghost, he's likely quite content too because it seems he's not alone. Anne told me, "Chris is often quite a serious little guy. He likes to be silly as much as the next kid but when he's serious about something there's no mistaking it. One day I was in the bathroom with him, cleaning him up before dinner. He looked over in the direction of the bathtub and, as calm as could be, said, 'There's a little girl in here.' Those words were no sooner out of his mouth than his eyes flew up to a spot directly above where he'd been staring and he said, 'Oh, look, now she's up near the ceiling.' I followed his sight line but I certainly couldn't see anything. I even tried looking in the mirror. There was absolutely no doubt, though, from Chris's behaviour, that he was looking at something that was very real to him."

Today, the spirited young family continues to thrive in their carefully chosen home, or perhaps we should say in the home that the spirits carefully chose for them.

CHAPTER 2
Transported to Beyond

Canada is an enormous country,
covering just less than ten million square kilometres.
Simply getting from one destination to another has
always been, and continues to be, an important factor in
Canadian life. This heritage has created its own legacy
of ghostly folklore.

Of course the fact that our huge country spreads
"from sea to glorious sea" means that we also have
a rich sea-fearing tradition.
The following ghost stories are all linked by the
common theme of travelling in or around Canada.

Legend of the Light

One of the most widely accepted ghost stories in western Canada is that of the St. Louis Light in Saskatchewan. Located about 40 kilometres (25 miles) south of Prince Albert and 100 kilometres (62 miles) north-northeast of Saskatoon, the small town of St. Louis has been drawing crowds to witness the phenomenon for generations.

The legend behind the supernatural sight has become somewhat blurred with the passage of years, but all versions connect the ghostly lights with a tragic railway accident. The train tracks are gone now, torn up many years ago. All that is left today is a flat stretch of land along which witnesses report seeing either the headlight of a spectral train or the lantern of an accidentally decapitated train worker.

Sightings of this phantom light are among the oldest and most consistent in Canada. Almost every time I take part in a nationwide phone-in radio show, at least one caller has an experience to relate about the eerie anomaly. During the Halloween 2000 edition of the CBC radio show "Midday Express," a man who had spent his teenage years in the Prince Albert area called to say that he and his friends went to St. Louis on a regular basis and saw the ghost lights almost every time.

Usually it was the same group of friends who made the trip but occasionally other people would join them. Frequently, when these newcomers saw the light they were skeptical and suggested that what they were seeing was simply a reflection of car headlights. This is a fairly common explanation, but it is easily disproved. Some believers point out that sightings of the light pre-date the time that cars came to the community. Others simply maneuver their own vehicles into all possible positions to show that the light is not a reflection.

Two young Edmonton-area filmmakers, Kim Brix and Derick Walsh, journeyed to St. Louis and arrived on a frosty cold evening in February 1996. They were producing a documentary about ghost stories and were determined to catch the eerie light on tape. En route, they discovered an additional ghostly legend when they were warned by townsfolk to keep an eye out for the phantom hitchhiker. They didn't see any hitchhiker, ethereal or corporeal, but they did see the light—briefly.

When they arrived at the site both Kim and Derick were eager to stretch their legs before setting up their camera equipment. The two young men stood behind the car and gazed, in a somewhat unfocused way, at the level piece of land nearby and leading off into the distance. As they did so, they could hardly believe their eyes. There, before them, exactly as people had described, was the phantom light. Unfortunately, although they rushed to start filming, the light extinguished just moments later and never reappeared again all night.

Many other people have had somewhat better luck than Kim and Derick. Details have been recorded of an entire roll of film being shot at what the photographer saw as the St. Louis Light. When he had the film developed every exposure was completely white, except for two small red dots on each photograph. No one has ever been able to offer an explanation for this oddity.

Dr. Terry Matheson, a professor of English at the

University of Saskatchewan, "has always been interested in paranormal phenomena." He was intrigued when, in the summer of 2000, his daughter told him about the anomaly visible near St. Louis.

Dr. Matheson explained, "My daughter told me of a strange light she had heard of in the small hamlet of St. Louis .... She was in charge of a group of exchange students from across Canada. Her superior, who had grown up in the area, mentioned that it might be fun and a bit of an adventure to take her people up to St. Louis and see if they could see the mysterious (but well known locally) light."

The man continued, "A few days after the excursion my wife and I invited my daughter and her troupe over for dinner, at which point she and her students told me excitedly that they had, in fact, seen the light. While believing them, I was of course, skeptical concerning the paranormal nature of the light, to say nothing of the authenticity of the ghost story that surrounded it."

As the author of *Alien Abductions: Creating a Modern Phenomenon*, a book that looks at the role authors of abduction books play "in shaping (and creating)" the stories, Matheson "was intrigued and as soon as my daughter had some spare time she took me out to 'see the light' as it were. Luckily, we had no trouble seeing it, and it lived up to her description in every respect."

One visit to the site of the ghost lights was not nearly enough for Dr. Matheson. "I returned home with my curiosity sufficiently aroused as to tell a friend and we drove up the next night, complete with my friend's camcorder. Again we were lucky, and we were able to take what I believe is some very impressive video footage of the phenomenon."

For those of us not able to see either the light or the video in person, the writer supplied a word picture. The light "is more or less as you have heard from other witnesses, although not quite as dramatic as the folklore would have it. The light begins—or at least it did both nights I saw it—by appearing as a faint glow apparently just behind the trees that border the abandoned rail line/now narrow pathway, on the right-hand side, seemingly on the horizon."

The man's detailed description continued. "The path [of the light] appears to rise to a height that seemed by a very rough estimate about 100 to 200 yards (90 to 180 metres), maybe less. It then seems to move to the centre of the path, whereupon it grows both in size and brightness, briefly reaching a magnitude considerably greater than, say, the planet Venus. As an amateur astronomer, I can state this with a degree of accuracy.

"The light is pure white initially. After reaching a peak of brightness, it quickly vanishes and is usually (but not invariably) replaced in a few seconds by a red light that is never more than a pinpoint of no discernible shape. This red light seems to wobble for a few seconds, then disappears, leaving blackness. A little while later, the phenomenon repeats itself, but not exactly as before. Each appearance had unique aspects and no two appearances were identical.

"As mentioned, it also takes on discernible size (from the original point of light when first seen) and, in magnification, looks remarkably like a light from an old-fashioned locomotive (doubtless accounting for the phantom railroad train in the various ghost stories that evolved over the years)," the English professor suggested.

removal of the remains ... from their place of interment on the banks of the Peel River to Fort Simpson" should be carried out. It was an enormous undertaking, for it meant disinterring the body from the frozen soil and travelling some 1300 kilometres (about 800 miles) by the only method of transportation available—dogsled. For the journey, the long-buried body had to be transferred out of its original casket into a considerably sturdier one.

Peers's coffin was pried opened as soon as it was unearthed. Although those gathered at the scene had no way of knowing it at the time, the condition they found the corpse in foreshadowed the eerie events that would follow. MacFarlane described the strange sight this way: "On being exhumed, the body was found to be in much the same condition which it had assumed shortly after the day of its burial." Seeing such a state of preservation must have been unnerving to the witnesses, perhaps especially so to the people who were then going to accompany the body at least part of the way to its final destination.

The difficult journey eventually began, "over the rugged masses of tossed-up ice which occur at intervals along the mighty Mackenzie River." By March 1860, the expedition had reached Fort Good Hope, "a distance of 300 miles [480 kilometres]." From there the trip became even more difficult. As the coffin, and the team's necessary provisions, rode on sleds behind dog teams, the accompanying men laboured along on snowshoes. By the time they reached Fort Good Hope, the men and animals were dangerously near complete exhaustion. MacFarlane realized that, if some changes weren't made, he, the dogs and the other couriers of the remains might all be as dead as their cargo.

They needed to lighten their load considerably but there was nothing they could safely dispense with—except the coffin containing Peers's body. And so, Peers's body was once again unceremoniously uncrated. The wooden box was left behind, leaving the body exposed but the load lightened. The body and its entourage were soon on their way once again.

The travellers rested again at Fort Norman, the next fort along the Mackenzie River, before starting out on the "last and longest portion of the journey." The trek's arduous schedule, as MacFarlane described it, is difficult to imagine in the twenty-first century. "We usually got under way by three or four a.m., dined at some convenient spot at noon and after an hour's rest resumed our journey until sunset when we laid up for the night, generally in a spruce bluff on the top of, or close to, the immediate riverbank." None of these conditions apparently troubled the men. They kept the dogs, supplies and the body near them throughout the nights. All was going much as planned until March 15, 1860, coincidentally the seventh anniversary of Peers's death.

As is often the case when a ghost is present, the animals noticed the change first. "The dogs began to bark," MacFarlane explained. Ignoring the noise, the men got on with setting up camp. First one man and then another began hearing a human voice—a human voice calling out a single word—"march."

"It seemed to have been uttered by someone at the foot of the bank who wished to drive away the dogs in his path. We all left our work in order to see who the stranger was, but no one appeared. The dogs surrounded the body at a distance of several feet, still apparently excited at something."

A haunted funeral procession under the northern sky.

Despite repeated attempts by their masters to soothe them, the agitated dogs would not be calmed. Then, without warning, as inexplicably as they became excited, the animals became quiet and peaceful again. The next day the beleaguered group set out again. All went well until three days later when the men "heard a loud call, twice repeated." They searched the area the voice seemed to have come from, near where they'd left the dog train carrying the body, but they could find nothing.

Early the next morning they set out on the last leg of their trip, arriving at Fort Simpson "on the afternoon of the twenty-first of March." The men completed their mission when "the body was duly coffined and buried in the Company's graveyard on the twenty-third of that month."

Once that chore was accomplished, the men began to chat with other traders and they told of the disembodied voice they had heard. One of the men listening to the tale had known Peers very well. He imitated the man's style of speech in ordering a team of dogs forward. "March," he said, in exactly the way it had been heard during the trek. MacFarlane said nothing but did wonder if it was the ghost of Augustus Richard Peers that had spoken.

That night, while staying at Fort Simpson, MacFarlane's musings were answered when Peers's ghost appeared in their room. MacFarlane related, "I became suddenly and over-poweringly conscious of what seemed to have been the spirit or supernatural presence of the late Mr. Peers. I instantly covered my face with the blanket and remained speechless."

MacFarlane was sharing the room he was sleeping in with another man. Each one felt the ghost come into the room but hid, in fear, at the first glimpse of the apparition. Even in 1913, fifty-three years after the experience, when MacFarlane wrote of his encounter with the ghost of his long-deceased colleague, he regretted having passed up what was, to him, clearly a chance to commune with the dead. He stated simply, "We missed our opportunity."

As for Peers, we must assume that his spirit rested calmly once it arrived in Fort Simpson, as it had for those seven years during which his earthly remains were interred at Fort McPherson. Apparently, it was the journey between the two posts that unsettled the ghost.

Ghostly Smoker

The story of Esau Dillingham's life is not a pretty one. He was probably born in the late 1800s, although exactly when and precisely where has long been forgotten. It is known for certain that by 1910, Dillingham was living in rugged, rural Labrador and that, by then, he was no longer called Esau Dillingham. People who dealt with the huge man simply knew him as "Smoker"—the word used to identify someone who made "moonshine" liquor. Hidden out in the bush, Smoker ran a still from which he made alcohol—deadly alcohol.

Spruce cones, sugar and yeast were the main ingredients in Smoker's hooch. Quality control was not assured, but nevertheless the man did a steady and highly profitable business. Some of his customers were more fortunate than others. Some went mad, some went blind. Others only became dreadfully ill, ill enough to wish—for a day or so, anyway—that they were dead. A few others did find the relief of death soon after ingesting Smoker's intoxicants.

Smoker's deadly trade had not gone unnoticed by the law, but he proved difficult to apprehend. He lived near his ever-productive still, and the area was surrounded by bear traps set to capture and immobilize anyone who came too close. When he had to travel throughout the snowy Labrador countryside, he camouflaged himself by wearing a coat of white fur and by driving a team of white dogs. Occasionally when he was out making his rounds, lawmen would spot him and give chase, but they inevitably lost sight

A dogsledding ghost lends a hand to lost travellers.

of Smoker as he sped away, blending in perfectly with the surrounding snowscape.

It wasn't until 1920 that Smoker's trade finally caught up to him. In a tragic sort of justice, the bootlegger began to imbibe his own concoctions, went mad and murdered a man who had come to his hideout to make a purchase. Near death himself by then, Smoker could not escape the law this time. He was arrested and taken to a jail cell at the Frenchman's Island police station. While there, perhaps as a result of an alcohol-induced seizure, Smoker broke his back. It's possible that he knew he was dying because, just hours later, Esau Dillingham found religion.

"Lord, I know I've been wicked, but I don't want to go to hell. Let me drive my team across this land until the end of time, so that I can undo the wrongs I've done," he prayed before breathing his last dying breath.

Not long afterward, a trapper trading at a nearby post had an amazing story to tell. He'd been driving his dog team through a raging blizzard when he realized that he had lost his way. The image of a "big man dressed all in white furs" suddenly appeared beside him, he told a trader. The unknown driver and his team guided the trapper to shelter before disappearing from view.

After that, reports of Smoker's ghost were told regularly. One of the most detailed and credible reports was of a sighting that took place in 1949. Two RCMP officers, George Bateson and Ed Riopel, were stationed at the Labrador outpost of Frenchman's Island. One winter's day they were returning, on dogsled, to the safety of their quarters. The wind picked up until it was fiercely blowing razor-sharp ice particles against the few centimetres of flesh exposed around the men's eyes. Snow blindness seemed inevitable; death by freezing would most certainly follow.

No one knows whether it was Bateson or Riopel who first saw the blurred image of a man driving a team of dogs. To the policemen, Smoker and his team were nothing more than barely visible dim shapes over to their right. They didn't know it at the time, but their saviour had arrived.

The officers called to the man, but he didn't respond. Realizing that they were doomed if left on their own, the pair began to follow. For two gruelling hours, the lawmen unknowingly followed the ghost of a deadly lawbreaker. The men's resources were near depletion when the wind subsided for just a moment and they caught a glimpse of a cabin with smoke coming from its chimney. The shelter wasn't far off in the distance. They could make it. They knew they would live.

When the curtain of white, blowing particles picked up again, their ghostly escort had vanished. Bateson and Riopel finished the last few metres of their trek on their own. The nearly frozen men were welcomed by the trappers who'd set up camp in the cabin. Once they had eaten and slept, the two officers told how they came to find themselves where they were.

"We must find out who it was who guided us here," Bateson told the listening men. "We owe him a great debt. He saved our lives."

"You'll never find that one on this side of the veil," a trapper replied enigmatically. "That was Smoker and he's been dead for nearly thirty years."

The two RCMP officers sat in stunned silence. Their lives had been saved by a ghost—the ghost of a repentant murderer. And so, a small portion of the circle of life had closed. Instead of evading the lawmen in the area, Smoker had saved them.

As far as anyone knows, the ghost of Smoker is still making good his deathbed entreaty. Even though his life was not an admirable one, this ghost story proves that his afterlife was most worthwhile.

On and Off the Road Again

Haunted or possessed cars are the stuff of fiction. Stephen King certainly did well with the premise through his eerie novel, *Christine*. While researching my book *Ghost Stories of Hollywood* I came across evidence that the car actor James Dean was driving when he was killed may also have been haunted. Six deaths can be directly connected to associations the victims had with that car.

Unfortunately for our peace of mind, haunted cars are not only in the realm of the famous, for ordinary folk too are sometimes involved. The Second World War had just ended and many Canadians looked forward with confidence to the future. A couple named Margaret and Albert in Calgary, Alberta were among them. Albert purchased a used 1932 Model B Ford. Although the car was in excellent shape, and a handsome-looking vehicle, Margaret took an immediate dislike to it. Nevertheless, to please her husband, she

The man who died in a 1932 Ford continued to haunt the car.

agreed to go for a drive in it. As they headed down a grade near the town of Cochrane, near Calgary, the brakes failed. Albert geared down as much and as quickly as he could, but still they plummeted downhill, passing other cars despite his attempts to slow the vehicle. In trying to avert disaster, Albert steered toward the side of the road. Seconds later the couple was sitting in a stationary car—in the middle of a slough.

It was then that Margaret confided her concerns. Right from the beginning, she'd sensed the ghost of a tall, thin, dark-haired man in the car. He died in the vehicle, she guessed, and would never leave it. Margaret begged her husband to sell the haunted car, but he would not hear of it—until the couple had to make an emergency trip from Calgary to the town of Gibbons just north of Edmonton. Unexpectedly, the steering wheel seemed to develop a mind of its own even though, when they stopped to have a mechanic check the mechanism, they were told there was nothing wrong.

On the trip home to Calgary, the car simply stopped and would not allow itself to be restarted. The couple had to spend their last money on a hotel room in which to spend the night. The next morning, they again had the car examined by a mechanic and again were told that there was nothing wrong with it.

Albert and Margaret finally did get home to Calgary but, by then, the transmission had also jammed and they were only able to drive in one gear. At this point, even Albert had had enough. After some investigation, they received information that confirmed Margaret's sense that a man had, in fact, died in the car. She explained, "His ghost had remained, still in control of the old Model B." Margaret added a postscript to the ghost story: "The dealer, under supervision, tore that car apart—forever."

Titanic

One ship, one deadly event in the history of shipping, will haunt our collective consciousness forever. I refer, of course, to the sinking of the "unsinkable" Royal Mail Ship *Titanic*. Since that fateful and fatal day—April 14, 1912—intensive and extensive investigations have been conducted into what actually happened, but no definitive answers have ever been found.

Were the series of events that led to the deaths of 1522 people inevitable? Could the *Titanic's* collision with the iceberg at the edge of Newfoundland's Grand Banks have been prevented? And was that deadly encounter caused by human error or, worse still, by human ego?

All that is known for certain is that the roots of this tragic tale are anchored in a time long before the cursed ship's date with infamy. Tendrils of evidence even creep back to a time prior to the days when executives with the White Star Line shipping company first conceived of their "Olympic class" line, a proposed set of three ships, all enormous and all to be named after a mythical race of giants. The *Titanic*, launched on April 10, 1912, was the second of the fleet to be produced.

It is a well-known fact of history that the luxurious liner left the British port of Southampton with 2227 people aboard—all alive and well. What is not as well known, however, is that deep in one of the ship's holds, *Titanic* also carried a body, the mummified body of an ancient Egyptian princess who had, in life, been an influential member of the menacing Cult of the Dead. Egyptologists estimated that this woman had lived and died around 1600 BCE, but evidence from early in the twentieth century indicated that her evil spirit continued to live on.

In 1910, Douglas Murray, an expert on ancient Egypt, was visiting Cairo. Just before he was scheduled to return to his home in England, Murray was approached by a sickly-looking American. Despite the stranger's unpleasant appearance, Murray couldn't resist transacting the business he proposed, for the dishevelled man was offering an exquisite artifact for sale at a very reasonable price. Without a moment's hesitation, the scholar issued a cheque to the American, and possession of the gold and enamel mummy case changed hands.

Ecstatic, Murray bragged about the wonderful deal he had made. When his colleagues warned him that the mummy was cursed, he scoffed at them, thinking their words were based only on disgruntlement brought about by envy. The Brit disregarded all of the warnings and set about making arrangements to ship home the newest addition to his collection, although Murray himself planned on staying in Egypt for some time. He and others were about to embark on a trip up the Nile. Just days after their journey began, Douglas Murray became the victim of a freak accident. The gun he was carrying exploded in his hand. Despite agonizing medical procedures, a few weeks later Murray's arm had to be amputated.

As soon as he was well enough to travel, the man arranged for passage home. Concerned that he might not be able to manage the trip alone, two of Murray's colleagues accompanied him. Both died, of unexplained causes, during the voyage. Perhaps the man's grief at his loss made him pay less than his usual amount of attention to his finances for, if he had taken the time to balance his bank account, Douglas Murray would have noticed that the cheque he had issued to pay for the mummy had not been cashed. The man who'd sold the "treasure" to Murray had died before he'd had a chance to cash the cheque issued to him.

Weeks later, the two specially trained shippers who'd travelled with the mummy on its voyage from Egypt to Britain died unexpectedly. Those deaths were enough for Douglas Murray. He was convinced now that what he been warned about was true—the spirit of the long-dead woman was not only active, but evil. He vowed to get rid of the encased mummy once and for all.

An English woman heard about the unusual object and decided that she wanted to own it. Although Murray tried to warn her of its dangers, she insisted. A short while later, the new owner not only was stricken with an undiagnosed illness, but was also grieving for her mother who had died unexpectedly, and was lonely for the lover who'd suddenly deserted her. Terrified, she tried to give the case back to Murray.

Murray wouldn't take it, but he passed the beautiful yet cursed coffin on to the British Museum. As part of the process of adding the gift to its collection, the museum had the case photographed. No sooner had the photos been taken than the photographer died. The next night, the museum supervisor, who'd ordered the pictures be taken, died in his sleep.

Not surprisingly, the press had become aware of this series of events. Writing about them made great copy and

The Titanic *preparing to leave England.*

sold vast numbers of newspapers. The publicity also served to warn the British Museum that it might be best served by shipping its newest display piece as far away as possible, and by the safest possible means. The curators had no interest in maintaining any further connection with the eerie article. No expense was spared as administrators made the shipping arrangements. The case, unopened, was packed in a cargo hold for the maiden voyage of a ship scheduled to leave Southampton port on April 10, 1912. That ship, of course, was the *Titanic.*

At this point, it would be folly to even guess as to whether or not the ancient evil spirit in the beautiful case was implicated in any way with the *Titanic's* lethal demise. It would be equally foolish, however, not to acknowledge that the presence of such a strong and clearly evil force might have had at least some negative impact on the events as they unravelled over the next five days.

In hindsight, many have said that even the launching of the *Titanic* gave indications that a malevolent power was at work aboard that ship. The first incident might have been intended as a warning, a warning that *Titanic's* experienced Captain E.J. Smith ignored. After all, Smith had been at the helm of the *Olympic* when it was launched. He knew that ʾe tremendous wake created by these new White Star Line ts could, and did, suck every ship near them directly eiʳ path. The force of the *Olympic* entering the har- ̣shed a smaller ship, the *Hawke*, up against the ̣ous one, seriously damaging both vessels.

That scene was nearly repeated when *Titanic* was launched. This time, Smith altered the course of the mammoth, while tugboats pulled a smaller ship, the *New York*, out of harm's way. Thus, having narrowly averted a catastrophe, the most luxurious ocean liner ever built slid out to sea at noon on Wednesday, April 10, 1912 and, just four days later, sailed into the annals of infamy.

Reams of information have been written about the *Titanic's* collision with the enormous berg of ice just moments after it had been sighted at 11:40 p.m. on April 14, 1912. Many people far more knowledgeable than I have offered extensive documentation of the awful events that followed. My purpose here is to remind you that the ship will always be connected with Canada. The *Titanic* sank onto the underwater Newfoundland Ridge, and many of the recovered bodies are buried in Canadian soil in Halifax, Nova Scotia. Oh yes, and aboard the *Titanic* was an ancient, evil, Egyptian mummy whose ghost is known to have left a trail of deaths in its ruinous wake.

And so, the eerie and deadly fate of the *Titanic* clearly began long before April 1912. Even as a story it did not begin then for, one night in 1898, a New York author named Morgan Robertson woke suddenly from a deep sleep. He'd had a terrible nightmare. The dream had been so lucid and so disturbing that he immediately jumped from his bed in an attempt to separate himself from its horrors. He paced his bedroom for a time but the dream images of a sinking ship and people helpless in the freezing water would not leave his mind. In an attempt to purge these thoughts, Morgan Robertson sat down at his writing desk and began to write out the details of the terrible nightmare that wa haunting him. He wrote feverishly until some of the fee ings of fright eased.

It was at that point that Robertson realized he had dreamed an entire story, a complete plot—beginning, middle and spectacular ending. In addition, the characters and their fates were riveting. He immediately set about formalizing what had been his middle-of-the-night scribblings. Soon a completed novel emerged.

He sold the manuscript to a Boston publisher for one hundred dollars. The book sold well enough but sales were certainly not spectacular. As a result, by spring of 1912, not many people had read his book about an enormous ocean liner called the *Titan*, a behemoth of 70,000 tons, 800 feet in length and carrying 2250 passengers. This fictitious ship, the *Titan*, was luxurious beyond any dream of that era

—any dream, that is, except Robertson's. He described the dream on which he based his novel.

"It was a wild April day ... the ship was at sea ... [she] was said to be unsinkable and was full of rich, complacent people ... great chandeliers shimmered and swayed ... an orchestra played ... I knew there was peril ahead ... I called to the captain to decrease speed, but he didn't ... an iceberg speared into her steep black side like a great fang and there was a terrible sound of breaking metal and people screaming and crying."

He went on, "There was also treasure aboard this ship. I knew all would be lost, that the lifeboats would take away the rich and influential, leaving the poor to a certain death. The ship's orchestra played on as the huge vessel sank, taking [her] architect down with [her]."

In 1912, when Robertson read of the imminent sailing of the *Titanic*, he immediately realized the eerie similarities between the ship of his dreams and the dream ship of the White Star Line. He began to draft a telegram to send to the company, warning them of the grave danger ahead. But then Robertson reconsidered his plan. The person receiving a telegram that read, "Cancel the *Titanic's* maiden voyage—I had a nightmare about it years ago" would surely disregard the message as having come from a lunatic.

And so, Morgan Robertson, whose dream and novel had foretold the sinking of the *Titanic*, did nothing. Sadly, his book, which he had titled *Futility*, sold very well after the terrible disaster at sea in 1912. Of course, the increased sales did not reflect a sudden appreciation of the man's writing style but of the strange predictive powers of his story, for Morgan Robertson, a mediocre novelist with no known psychic powers, had predicted the worst sea-going accident of all time.

As a postscript to this well-known story, I shall quote directly from a Canadian newspaper, the *Edmonton Daily Bulletin*. In its Tuesday, July 23, 1912 edition—more than three months after Captain E.J. Smith of the *Titanic* had died in the icy waters of the North Atlantic—the headline of an article stated: "HE SAYS HE SAW AND TALKED TO CAPT. SMITH." The subhead continued, "Montreal Mariner, Retired, Swears That He Met and Spoke to the Commander of the Ill-Fated *Titanic* in Baltimore."

Giving a placeline of Baltimore, Maryland, and a date-line of July 22, the article went on to report:

> Peter Pryal, of Montreal, a wealthy retired mariner of this city, declared by his physician to be perfectly sane, swore today that he saw and talked with Captain Smith, of the *Titanic*, on Thursday morning. Pryal was a shipmate and close friend of Captain Smith for seventeen years.
>
> Late Wednesday morning the mariner swears he saw Captain Smith of the *Titanic* approaching him. Walking up to him, he said, "Captain Smith, how are you?"
>
> Then, according to Pryal, the man answered: "Very well, Pryal; but please don't delay me; I am on business."
>
> Pryal followed Smith, the chase ending at a railroad station, where Smith purchased a ticket for Washington. As he passed to board a car he turned to Pryal and said: "Goodbye, shipmate, until we meet again."

Pryal is a total abstainer and swears he is telling the truth. He says Smith was probably saved through Providence and was then afraid to face the world.

Captain Smith's nephew lives in Baltimore, but no one has seen him [the nephew] for several days.

Does that article describe one of the final eerie mysteries associated with the *Titanic*? According to all witnesses, Captain E.J. Smith did as he was supposed to: he went down with his ship and, like hundreds of others that night, died horribly, either by drowing or by freezing to death in the North Atlantic. Did his understandably restless spirit somehow return to our earthly plane as a ghostly guardian of sorts, perhaps to strive to avert other such disasters? Maybe these questions should just be added to the long list of unknowns surrounding one of the twentieth century's most haunting tragedies.

The Voice

Not all ghosts are visual images. Some spirits come to us as mere whiffs of a fragrance, or, as in the story that follows, simply a sound, a voice.

The year was 1889. The place was St. Martins Bay, New Brunswick. Young Jack Dyre had been hired to help crew a ship christened the *Union*. Dyre loved the sea and looked forward to many adventures aboard the freighter but, like most of us, Jack worked to earn money. When the opportunity came up, therefore, to earn a little extra cash, he jumped at the chance—especially since the assignment seemed to be an easy one.

The *Union's* captain and three other crew members all wanted to go ashore for a night, but someone needed to stay aboard the ship. Before long, the group had negotiated an arrangement and everyone was happy. Jack would have a little extra in his pay packet and the other four men could enjoy some shore leave.

Because there was little to do aboard the docked vessel, Jack decided to go to bed early but, just before he did, he made one final check of the vessel. All was secure and quiet; the man fell into his bunk and was asleep in no time.

Not long after, Jack Dyre woke up with a start. He sat straight up in bed, sure that he had heard someone call out his name. Worse, this voice warned him to leave the ship immediately. Although he was badly frightened, Jack knew he had to get out of bed and find the trespasser who had come on to the boat and spoken to him. Despite a thorough search of a vessel he knew well, Jack could not find anyone on board nor anything unusual anywhere in the ship. Relieved, he returned to his bed where, after tossing and turning for a few minutes, he fell back to sleep.

Just as he had drifted off into a deep sleep, the voice came again. "Jack Dyre, you must leave this ship now." Even more terrified this time, Jack sat shivering in bed, the covers pulled up around him, trying to get up the courage to do what he knew he had to do—check once again for an intruder aboard the ship.

Moments later, all the while talking out loud to himself, Dyre rose from his secure bunk and once again inspected the ship, this time even more carefully. This second search netted no more of a solution to the origin of the strange message than the first one had. Badly confused and frightened, he returned to his bed but he knew falling asleep would be impossible.

As he lay awake, pleading silently and futilely for morning to come quickly, he heard the voice again. "Jack Dyre, you must leave this ship now."

By daybreak, Dyre had had enough of staying aboard the spooky ship with voices that seemed to come from nowhere bearing scary messages. He was packed and ready to leave the ship as soon as his captain returned. The frightened man had no idea what or who could have spoken to him overnight. He just knew for certain that he would never set sail on that vessel again.

Although the *Union's* captain tried very hard to change his sailor's mind, Dyre was gone, and the captain knew that a replacement worker would have to be found before they could set out again. There were dozens of other young men on the docks who wanted adventure so he had no trouble hiring someone. The *Union*, her core of senior crew and one new man, sailed out of the port by noon.

The captain could tell right away that this trip was not going to be a fast one. There was almost no wind and any progress the ship did make was related to the action of the tide. Once well out into St. Martins Bay, the wind died down completely. The *Union* and dozens of other ships were completely becalmed.

As experienced sailors, those stranded on the still waters of the bay simply set about swabbing the decks and shining the brass on their ships, waiting for the wind to pick up. For the *Union*, however, that time really never did come. As she rested on the water's calm surface, the ship overturned. The captain and one crew member were rescued. The man who took Jack Dyre's place was among the three whose bodies were never recovered.

And so, it would seem that heeding the phantom voice that had persisted in warning him throughout the previous night had saved Jack Dyre's life.

Regina's Demise

In waters almost due north of Tobermory, in Ontario's Georgian Bay, lies at least one haunted island, Cove Island. Records show that a well-experienced captain by the name of Tripp was sailing a slightly old and decaying schooner, the *Regina*, near Cove Island on a beautiful September's day in 1881.

All would've been well for Captain Tripp, his crew and the *Regina* had the vessel's payload not been salt. As the heavily laden craft made her way from the port at Goderich into the waters of the bay, a wind blew up, and waves began crashing over the rotting deck. The wooden planks were no

Lighthouse or fright house?

longer sealed the way they once had been, and the water was leaking into the holds.

Had the cargo not been salt, the tragedy might never have occurred. The salt soaked up probably a hundred times its own weight, straining every seam and lowering the hull deeper and deeper into the water. Tripp's crew panicked and abandoned ship. Tripp stayed on board attempting to manage the craft by himself.

When the inevitable wreck of the *Regina* was found she rested against the rocks of Cove Island, her mast still visible above the surface of the water. Oddly, Captain Tripp's body was missing. Some say his remains were found by a search party and secretly buried in an unmarked grave on Cove Island. A ghost story that has been told since seems to support that theory.

One stormy night years later, the lighthouse keeper at Cove Island deserted his post. It was fully a decade later before the man was willing to admit that he had fled in terror after being confronted with the ghost of Captain Tripp.

Ghostly Presence

Ghost stories are many things, but it would seem self-evident that, by their very nature, they are extraordinary tales about the spirit or soul of someone who has died. In my years of collecting paranormal stories, I have come across only two about the spirits of people who are still alive. One of these tales is relayed below, and after reading it you might be even more puzzled than ever about this strange world we inhabit.

Icebergs off the eastern banks of Newfoundland have always been lethal threats to sailors and their ships. In late autumn of 1823, the captain of a square-rigged barque guided his vessel through the final hours of a voyage from Liverpool, England. It had been a difficult passage. Provisions were low and the crew was exhausted but, at last, the craggy shores of home were not far off.

About noon, the captain and his mate, Robert Brace, a young man from Torbay, Newfoundland, bundled up against the cruel cold and walked out onto the ship's deck. The freezing air all but took their breath away, so the two were silent as they made their routine navigational observations and checks. Once they were back in the captain's quarters, the men conversed comfortably, compared their assessments and worked out the ship's position and progress.

The skipper, as the older man was affectionately known, left Brace working and went to perform duties elsewhere on the ship. Brace hadn't heard his superior leave the room and so was not surprised to see, out of the corner of his eye, that the man was sitting at his desk, hunched over his writing slate, probably figuring out coordinates.

Finishing what he had to do in the captain's quarters, Brace turned to confirm his own figures with the ones the more experienced sailor had determined. The only problem was that the man sitting at the desk was not Robert Brace's captain. It was a stranger, a person Robert had never seen before.

This can't be, Robert tried to assure himself. *We've been at sea for days. No one could have come aboard this ship and no one could have remained hidden as a stowaway for this length of time.*

Brace called out to the man at the desk, demanding that he identify himself. The image remained silent but lifted his head from the slate he had been writing on and looked at Robert Brace with eyes as cold as the North Atlantic seas that were buffeting the barque.

Brace's knees quaked, sweat poured from his face. For moments, he was paralyzed with fear but, as soon as he was able to make his legs respond to his will, he ran to find the skipper.

"Who's in your cabin writing at your desk?" Brace demanded when he found the officer.

"No one is there, as far as I know," the man replied, in surprise. Robert Brace was one of his most trusted sailors. The captain didn't expect him, of all people, to be upset over some foolishness.

"There is a man sitting at your desk," Brace insisted.

"It must be one of the crew then, the second mate or possibly the steward. None of the others would go into my quarters without my permission."

"The man sitting at your desk and writing on your slate is no member of this crew. I have never seen this man before in my life, and yet he's aboard this ship," Brace exclaimed, trying to supply as many details as he could so that the captain would see the situation was unique and urgent.

Not wanting to call his most trusted worker a liar, the ship's leader pointed out the obvious—"We've been at sea for nearly six weeks. Where could he have come from?" Then, realizing that his mate was well aware of these facts, the skipper added, "Let's go below and find out."

The captain and the mate made their way back down to the quarters where Brace had seen and spoken to the stranger. The room was empty. Nothing seemed to be out of place, nothing was missing. At first, it seemed as though no one had been in the room at all—until Robert Brace noticed a message written in unfamiliar handwriting on the slate which had been left atop the captain's desk. The words "Sail for the northwest" had been neatly written across the surface.

"Did you write this?" the skipper asked Brace.

"No, of course not," he replied. "You know what my handwriting looks like. It doesn't resemble this script at all. Did you write it?"

The captain apparently felt that last question did not even warrant an answer, for he simply turned and left the room. Nearly half an hour elapsed before he returned.

"I've checked the handwriting of everyone on the ship. None of them write this way. I make the assumption that we have a stowaway and I've ordered a complete search of the ship," the older man informed Brace.

Although the crew searched the ship from port to starboard and bow to stern, they found no one. The captain was puzzled because he knew that Robert Brace was not the kind of man to make up a story about a stranger; besides which, the message on the slate seemed to back Brace's otherwise fantastic claim. The leader saw no alternative but to investigate what this strange series of events could mean. To that end he ordered the ship's helmsman to steer to the northwest.

With all hands on deck, the ship veered in a new direction—the direction indicated by the mysterious message. Everyone on board was acting as a lookout—they just weren't sure what they were looking out for. After an hour on the new route, no one had sighted anything unusual. It was the same after two hours—the seascape was more and more heavily dotted with icebergs but, other than those, the men spotted nothing out of the ordinary.

They'd been sailing on their new course, ninety degrees northwest from the old one, for three hours before they spotted what appeared to be the remains of a ship stuck fast in an ice field. When they approached as near as they dared, the sailors on the barque, Robert Brace included, could see that the trapped vessel was badly damaged. She was certainly not seaworthy and may actually have been abandoned.

Not knowing whether they were now on a rescue mission or on a salvage operation, the captain dispatched a trio of men, including Robert Brace, in a lifeboat to approach the stranded ship more closely. As they came nearby, they could hear voices. People were obviously still aboard. When members of the party in the lifeboat called out, their cries were answered by men scrambling around to the side of the deck nearest the approaching craft.

Waving madly, the men aboard the icebound vessel clearly indicated they both needed and wanted help.

"Thank God you're here," a figure from the deck shouted. "We couldn't have held out much longer. We're in imminent danger of sinking."

The rescue party steered the lifeboat over to a flat portion of a berg. The endangered sailors clambered down from their ship, crossed the ice, and then boarded the rescuer's boat. As was fitting, the captain of the abandoned craft spoke first.

"We left Liverpool weeks ago, bound for Quebec. We'd been stuck between those ice floes for so long that we'd all but given up hope of being rescued. We owe you our lives. How did you happen to be navigating this exact course?" the rescued leader inquired.

"Bring your men below where it's warmer," Robert Brace suggested. "We'll explain as best we can once we're in quarters."

Brace greeted the men with a nod as they eventually made their way below the barque's main deck and out of the elements. Several had passed by when Brace saw him— the man who had been sitting in the captain's quarters writing on the slate, writing the words that caused the decision to change course and, as a result, to find the marooned men. Brace stopped the sailor and asked, "Have you ever been aboard this vessel before?"

"No, of course, not," the confused, cold and badly shaken man replied.

"But, I've seen you," said Brace. "I know I have. It was earlier today, just after noon. You were sitting at the captain's chair, writing on his slate. Then you disappeared and we couldn't find you anywhere on board, but we did find your instructions to change our course. That's how we happened to spot your stranded ship," Brace explained.

"It could not have been me that you saw. Just after noon today, I was in my bunk trying to sleep. I don't think I ever lost consciousness completely. I did have a strange dream, although I can't recall its nature. Until a few minutes ago, I'd been aboard the same ship since we left Liverpool," the stranger informed Brace.

"But even the other man's clothes were the same as yours," Brace muttered in astonishment before he went to find his captain. He'd have to explain the situation, although he had no idea how he'd do so without looking like a fool.

The captain listened more patiently than Brace expected. He said nothing, but took a spare slate down from a shelf and handed it to the stranger saying, "Humour me, please. Write something on this slate—write 'Sail for the northwest.'"

The man was clearly puzzled, but did what he was asked and then handed the slate back to the captain who, in turn, compared it to the slate that had been on his desk when Brace had reported seeing someone or something writing on it. The handwriting was identical.

A stunned silence pervaded the room and then the man who had written the lifesaving message on the slate—twice—spoke. "Now I think I remember a snippet of my dream. I saw myself boarding another ship and pleading for help."

Somehow, the desperate man's mind had transported his spirit to the only possible chance for rescue. His spirit, his presence, his ghost, if you will, had travelled on a lifesaving mission—before, and to prevent, his own death.

Spectral Ships

Spectral ships, phantom ships, ghost ships, Flying Dutchmen. Even considered from my office on the Canadian prairies, these are fascinating and eerie. For some living near our country's coastlines, these supernatural vessels are a more immediately frightening and all-too-real element of life. Sightings of ships that sailed the world's oceans many years ago, especially those known to have come to a tragic end, have been reported for centuries, and from all over the world. Over the years, phantom ships have so captivated people's minds that books, songs, movies and even operas have been written around them.

The ghostly apparition of a spectral ship may take one of many forms. Some reports describe a pillar or a ball of fire on the water where, in reality, no such a presence could possibly be. Witnesses of other sightings report that they have stood helplessly on the shore and, in their own dimension of time, watched in horror as sailors scurry across a ship's blazing deck in panic before jumping, with agonizing screams, into the frigid seas and to certain death.

Still other accounts tell of seeing an old-fashioned sailing craft, clearly from another point in history, impossibly, but undeniably, scudding through the waves. The images are most often either dull grey or misty white, although some sailing phantoms glow with a supernatural luminescence. Whatever form the sighting takes, it seems that the long-ago perished ship has been doomed to replay its last, deadly moments on an eternal psychic loop.

Royal apparition: a man who would be king saw this imaginary ship.

As with other types of ghostly legends, stories about phantom ships can include a morality lesson. In the story of the original *Flying Dutchman*, history records that sometime in the 1700s, a Dutch captain named Van Straaten (or Van der Decken) stubbornly persisted in an attempt to sail around Africa's Cape of Good Hope, known as the Cape of Storms, for good reason. Continuing to navigate around the point, rather than waiting for calmer seas, meant sailing directly into the path of a life-threatening storm. The *Flying Dutchman* and all aboard her were lost in the storm, reminding everyone who hears the tale, and takes it to heart, that it is deadly to put one's own pride ahead of concern for the well-being of others, especially when such arrogance flies in the face of nature's power.

Over the years, many sailors have reported witnessing the *Flying Dutchman* foundering in the buffeting waves. Likely the most famous sighting of that ghost ship was made by the man who was later King George V. On June 11, 1881, while serving aboard HMS *Inconstant*, Prince George, as he was then known, and the rest of that ship's crew saw the ancient illusion plying the waves into eternity.

The *Young Teazer*

"There's the *Young Teazer*," people standing on the shores of Nova Scotia's Mahone Bay still call out. While there's a very good chance that the surprised witnesses are actually seeing the spectral remains of a ship that exploded and burned in the summer of 1813, it's almost equally possible that these folks are misnaming the fiery, floating phantom. The story of the *Teazer's* ghost may be the best known, but it is not the only legend of a ghost ship in that breathtakingly beautiful inlet.

First-hand accounts collected from long-time residents around the bay by the late author and folklorist Dr. Helen Creighton indicate that some sightings of a flaming rig are misidentified as the *Young Teazer*. An examination of the area's history reveals that more than enough trauma has occurred there to have left many scars on the surrounding psychic landscape. Storms have always been a risk to sailors on Mahone Bay, but pirates were also a very real and lethal threat in the 1800s. It would seem that the ghosts of these ocean-going thieves have remained behind to, occasionally, give folks of today some lessons in history.

The oddly named *Young Teazer* (there were two ships with the same name; this one was built later than the original *Teazer*) was actively pirating when she was hopelessly "cornered" by a much larger British ship sent to fight in the War of 1812. The captain of the doomed *Teazer* had far too much pride to allow himself, his ship or any of his men to be apprehended. Perhaps with his crew's agreement, perhaps not, he ignited a powder keg aboard the rig. The mammoth explosion that resulted burned for hours afterward. There are even those who say that, on some other plane of existence, the inferno still burns today. Those who make that claim have seen the image. As if seeing a flaming wreck from beyond would not be disturbing enough, its sighting has long been taken as a forecast of an imminent severe storm in the bay area.

Sightings of the *Teazer* are especially interesting because, while several people might be gathered at the same spot on the shoreline, some will see the image clearly and others not at all. Perhaps not everyone is equally blessed, or cursed, with the ability to detect such ghostly resonations from the past.

Of course, those who know historic ships well are able to identify the spectre they're seeing with certainty. Those with less knowledge might easily mistake other phantoms on the bay for the pirate ship. For instance, more than a hundred years later, an oil tanker caught fire and sank near Westerhaver's Point. This deadly blaze has also been seen many times over the years. When it is replayed, it has, sometimes, been misidentified as a sighting of the *Teazer*.

The pirates' ghosts still guard their treasure.

Other maritime apparitions that continue to play out as some sort of a double exposure—their time superimposed on ours—seem to be more aggressive. Many years ago, Joseph Hyson, a lifelong resident of the area, explained that ships and crews clearly from another era have followed more modern-day sailors, sometimes for hours, even right to shore. There were other instances reported by flesh-and-blood sailors who were so curious about a spectre they'd spotted that they rowed out to meet the ghostly vessel. Time and time again, the phantom ship would stay its course for shore, leading the investigators to believe they'd seen the ghosts of long-dead pirates intent on protecting their buried treasure.

These sightings still occur, and if you're visiting picturesque Mahone Bay and you see a ship from a bygone era—whether it's the *Young Teazer* or not—it might be wise to prepare for a fierce storm within the next twenty-four hours.

Ghost of the Baie

Some Canadian ghost stories are so old that it's easy for anyone to doubt their veracity. It's tough, though, for even the most skeptical to maintain their disbelief in the face of an in-person encounter—an actual sighting of the manifestation upon which a piece of folklore is based. That is exactly what William and Jean Robinson, who toured the Maritime provinces on their honeymoon in 1981, experienced. Westerners by birth, the couple wanted to explore a different part of the country.

Their marriage and honeymoon trip had been planned for autumn in order to coincide with the famous fall colours of the eastern seaboard. But the brilliance of the landscape, which they had so counted on enjoying, was not the most memorable sight they beheld on their journey, for they also saw something that neither of them thought could actually exist. On the evening of October 5, 1981, the Robinsons, like many people before and since, saw and heard the Phantom Ship of Baie des Chaleurs, New Brunswick.

"It was windy, the bay was turbulent," Jean began. "I couldn't guess how far away the flaming ship was because there were no markers from which to get a perspective. I just know the flames shot up; they seemed as high as they would've been if a building had been on fire. And they covered a large area."

William added, "We were spellbound by the sight. It didn't stay constant but would flare up and then subside. At first, neither of us could figure out what we were seeing, but, when the flames were the brightest, they illuminated an outline of an old-fashioned sailing ship. [The ship] was moving slowly toward land. Somehow, though, it wasn't the sight of the image that I found the most amazing part of the experience. It was that we could hear burning coals, and timbers, hissing as they were extinguished by the waves. We'd heard the folklore about people seeing ships that had sunk many years before. We never expected to see one though, because neither of us really believed that the stories were true. To not only see this spectre, but to hear it too was something we will never, ever forget."

The identity of the ghost ship is not known for certain, but there have been reports of the burning hulk on the waters separating New Brunswick from the Gaspé Peninsula since the 1800s. Some marine historians believe that the psychic imprint on the seascape is a French vessel that went missing in 1760. That vessel matches witnesses' reports over the years—a three-masted, square-rigged coal carrier.

Profoundly affected by their paranormal encounter, the Robinsons researched the history of the legend. They found that sometimes the apparition lasts for only minutes; other times, for hours. Not everyone sees it as a ship. Some say it is an inexplicable ball of flame. Others describe it as a column of fire. Their most striking research find was a description even more detailed than their own experience.

William recounted, "We read that, in 1892, a man named Richard Jefferson had been working aboard a train. As he glanced out across the bay, Jefferson noted, 'Smoke was billowing up through the rigging. Figures were rushing to and fro on her decks.' I guess the man panicked and called to the locomotive engineer. That man must've seen the strange sight before because Jefferson wrote that his superior merely shouted back at him, 'Hell, that's just the Burning Ship.' Moments later, the image apparently became obscured in a cloud of steam or smoke and then sank into the frigid waters."

This archival documentation reassured both William and Jean, who have never been able to erase the sight that had reached across the bay, and across time, as they stood on the shore and gazed upon the legendary Burning Ship.

Fire Upon the Water

The spectral pyrophenomenon seen on the waters dividing Prince Edward Island from the mainland Maritime provinces is, not surprisingly, known as the Phantom Ship of Northumberland Strait. We know this ghost story to be very old, by Canadian standards, because the Micmac advised European immigrants about the illusion, calling it "fire upon the water." Those familiar with the history of the area think the phantom dates back to the 1700s when a ship carrying Europeans immigrating to the New World burned and sank under the waters of Northumberland Strait.

The first written account was recorded in 1880 by the crew of a tugboat. Certain they had seen a fast-moving ship just outside of the harbour at Pictou, Nova Scotia, they headed out to offer aid. As the smaller boat made her way across the water, the image vanished. Confused, but still concerned, the tug's captain stayed his course. When they reached the spot where the flaming ship had disappeared, they found nothing—no survivors, no casualties, no floating pieces of a shipwreck—nothing.

When people are able to approach the manifestation, they speak of a large vessel, with three masts, her sails set. The image moves very fast in an easterly direction. It is often so real looking that witnesses summon the authorities, and once, in the late 1970s, several members of the RCMP detachment in Pictou were called out and also viewed the supernatural event.

A much more recent report is also possibly the most dramatic one connected with this Phantom Ship. The passengers of a powerful motorboat saw the vessel and gave chase, determined to catch what they were sure was the famous Phantom Ship. Their determination rewarded them with an experience to tell their grandchildren: they caught up to the phantom and were travelling so fast and with such unwavering direction that, in the words of one on board the small craft, "soon we were inside a ghostly glow and, as our motorboat kept going, we passed right through the Phantom Ship and saw it disappear behind us."

Pacific Presences

Canada's western coastal waters do not seem to be as haunted as the eastern shores, but some marine manifestations have been observed on the Pacific Ocean off the coast of British Columbia.

In my earlier book *Ghost Stories and Mysterious Creatures of British Columbia*, I tell the story of a phantom ship called the *Valencia*, which foundered on rocks just off B.C.'s rugged coast in 1906. Her image is still occasionally seen. Those who have the misfortune to have seen it are haunted by the memory for years afterward. These people consistently describe watching the ghosts of passengers and crew replaying their final seconds of life, clinging to the riggings as the doomed vessel is battered mercilessly by the ocean's raging waves.

Another story from that book describes an encounter by a Japanese freighter in 1957. While sailing on the Strait of Georgia en route to Seattle, the crew on the *Meitetsu Maru* spotted a fishing boat, ablaze, not far away. The freighter's captain ordered his sailors to approach the craft in distress, but, as they rowed closer to the smaller vessel, they could see that no one was left on board. They took note of as many official markings on the boat as were left visible and reported the wreck to authorities. Despite an intensive five-day search, no trace of the craft was ever found. Stranger still, no documents existed to indicate that any vessels were unaccounted for, at least not from that era.

A less well-known sighting also occurred on the Strait of Georgia, between Vancouver Island and B.C.'s mainland coast.

It was July 1934 and the *Mary Ann*, a privately owned pleasure craft, was navigating from Alaska to Seattle. Fog is not uncommon in the area and, as any experienced sailors would, those sailing the *Mary Ann* slowed and sounded their foghorn when the thick mist rolled in and surrounded their vessel.

When the fog lifted some hours later, those same sailors were startled to find an old wreck of a vessel hard up against their own starboard bow. The *Mary Ann's* captain knew he had to respond immediately or a collision would be imminent. Veering as tightly as he could to port, he may have said a silent prayer that his maneuver would be sufficient to avert disaster. He'd done what he could; all that was left was to wait and see how the potential catastrophe would play itself out.

The man may have had some possible scenarios in his mind, but what happened next made him disbelieve his own eyes. His turn was not acute enough to avoid a collision between his boat and the dilapidated old craft in its path. He watched in amazement as the *Mary Ann's* bow cut completely through the derelict he'd tried so hard to avoid hitting. Impossibly, this event occurred in complete silence. That was the captain's first clue that the boat he had just struck was not from the present.

Not understanding what had just happened, but grateful that no harm had come to his crew, himself or his craft, the captain gave orders to regain their original route. As he did he quickly belayed those orders, for he could now see a tugboat pulling a log boom straight ahead of his original course. If the ghostly guardian, a phantom navigational hazard, had not caused him to change his course, the *Mary Ann* would have plowed straight into a very real, and very deadly, navigational hazard.

Jane Miller of the Bay

Even Canada's Great Lakes are haunted. In my book *Ontario Ghost Stories*, I describe the continued sightings of ships such as the *Griffon*, the *Bannockburn* and the *Edmund Fitzgerald*, all of which sunk many years ago.

Even on Georgian Bay, which makes up the eastern portion of Lake Huron, a phantom occasionally makes an appearance. It's identified as the *Jane Miller*, a steamer that foundered in a raging blizzard with twenty-eight souls aboard on November 25, 1881. She was making her way across Colpoy's Bay and that's where she's usually seen, in weather similar to that in which she went down.

Twenty-eight souls still haunt the bay.

One of the largest groups to encounter this phantom ship were hunters who had camped on White Cloud Island. In the evening the quiet night air was punctuated with the eerie sounds of cries and moans. The men described the sounds as rolling off a certain area of the murky black nighttime waves in the bay. Despite straining their eyes, none of the men saw even an outline of an image.

These men, though used to roughing it in the outdoors, were shaken by what they'd heard. None of them slept that night and all were eager to leave the spot in the morning. As they sailed away in their boat the hunters were puzzled by a patch of oil on the water—oil that seemed to bubble up from the depths of the bay—in roughly the spot the dreadful cries had been heard the night before.

Like all ghost stories, tales of spectral ships have been found in historical and contemporary accounts, all around the world. The legends retold in this chapter are but a few of those found on Canadian waters.

CHAPTER 3
Spirit Snippets

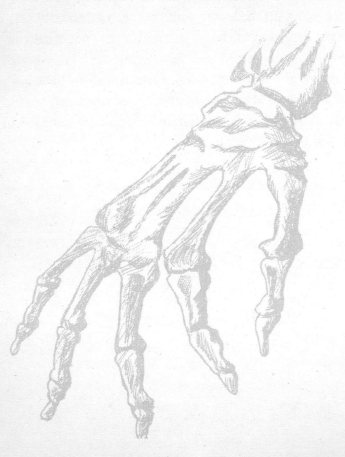

The following stories were all told to me by callers to various phone-in shows on radio stations. Because time is so limited during these calls and because the location is so well known to the caller, and completely unknown to me, I often end up with the story but sometimes not a description of the precise place where it occurred. Most of the following stories, however, are from western Canada and all are spooky representations of Canadians' experiences with the supernatural.

While listening to these callers recount their experiences, I always find it just a bit chilling that, no matter if the incident took place ten or more years ago, the callers' voices still betray the depth of emotion the people felt during the paranormal encounter.

A woman named Pat who called Bill Turner's show on CKLQ in Brandon, Manitoba, had this tale to relate.

"At the end of September 1998, my husband was quite ill and scheduled for surgery. The doctors were sure it was cancer. Of course, I was very upset about it and since one son is a truck driver and on the road and the other son lives in Halifax, I was home alone.

"I was standing at the kitchen sink doing dishes, it was about 9:00 p.m. and I was talking on the telephone to my sister-in-law in British Columbia. All of a sudden, I felt as if someone was standing behind my right shoulder and I gasped. I told my sister-in-law that I had to go and would call her back.

"I turned my head to see if there was anyone there and, there was!" Pat's next words were a statement but her inflection and tone made them sound as though she was questioning herself. "It was a person, in a brown robe like a monk's and the hood was up. I could not see a face. This person put a hand on my right shoulder and shook its head 'no.' Then, it just turned and walked toward the door and disappeared.

"I felt as if a great weight had been lifted off my shoulders. I knew that my husband would be okay, that 'they' didn't want him in 'their' world yet."

Pat was correct in her interpretation of the event, and the ghostly visitor had been a good predictor, for the woman's husband recovered from his illness. The reassuring image has never visited Pat again.

A ghostly visitor with a message

A man called to relay this next story of a house in rural southern Manitoba. He recalled, "The wife and I we moved into town from the farm about twenty-five years ago. [We] bought a little house along the highway [from a man whose] wife had died in the house."

Right from the start, the new owners detected something unusual about the place. "We'd be sitting watching TV and you could hear somebody walking upstairs. We knew there was no one there."

Despite these apparently contradictory circumstances, the couple was not overly disturbed but thought the ghost of the woman who had lived and died in the house was making the noise. As a result, the man explained, "We never paid much attention to it."

The ghost of the former owner was not content with just walking around. "We used to go out to the farm and always [left the] radio on. We'd come back and the radio would be off. I'd say to the wife, 'Did you shut the radio off?'"

His wife would always reply in the negative, so the couple figured it was just another ghostly prank. Perhaps to test their theory they decided to alter the process. "One time we left [the radio] turned off and when we came back [it] was on."

Turning the radio on and off was not the only attention-getter their resident ghost performed. "The wife had a couple of candlestick holders sitting on a china cabinet and I'll tell you, if it happened once it happened a dozen times. The candlestick holders would be sitting on the floor.

There's no way that they could fall off, [land] upright and not break." But that is exactly what these ornaments did.

Another time the couple was out, "getting the groceries one day. We came home, opened the door and we could hear the piano, someone pinging away on the piano. We thought our granddaughter had come into town so we said something and [the music] stopped. There was nobody at the piano. That happened twice [and] lots of times we'd come home and see that the cover on the piano keys had been lifted up."

This particular haunting had an unusual ending, the caller explained. "My wife passed away five years ago, quite suddenly, and I never heard a thing from that ghost, [but] now this is a little strange, I woke up in the middle of the night and it seemed like somebody had turned all the lights on in the living room, the dining room and the kitchen. It was a real bright light but it wasn't like the lights from the ceiling or anything, it was just kind of a bright light. I got up and went out and there was somebody standing in the doorway [between] the kitchen and the living room. I could see the outline of this person. I said 'Oh.' It just faded away and the whole house went dark. I didn't recognize the person at all."

The man continued, "One other night I got up and I was sitting on the edge of the bed. The kitchen and the living room started to get light and I looked and here's this person, I could see the outline of a person sitting beside me. To this day nobody can tell me any different. I think it was my wife [because she] and I we used to go for car rides and when we were driving down the road I used to reach over, grab her by the knee. She'd just say, 'What are you trying to do?' or something like that. That night, when I was sitting on the edge of the bed, I reached over to put my hand on her knee, well, this person's knee, and that person said, 'You can't do that anymore.' The room went dark and it was gone. It happened, I know it did." The caller acknowledged that the experiences were "scary at times" but concluded with the assurance that "for this past two years I haven't heard or felt a thing."

Perhaps both women who lived in the house on the highway have now gone on to their final rewards.

A man named Jake called to say that when he lived in an apartment in south Calgary he witnessed something that he still cannot explain. "I had three little china figurines, three little penguins, that used to sit on top of my television. The penguin in the centre, the thing was only about maybe 2½ or 3 inches tall [7.5 centimetres] and, on a fairly regular basis, the thing would just fly off the TV and come out about 2 or 3 feet [about 1 metre] into the living room."

If this activity weren't strange enough, he further clarified, "It never broke, it landed on the carpet. It didn't come off the top of the TV with a lot of force, I'm not saying it floated over, more like a soft lob. We lived there for just under a year and it would happen at least once a month."

Whatever it was that threw the ornament did not move when Jake did. "I've still got the penguin. When we moved into our house I was kind of waiting to see if it would do the same thing but it's just been sitting there on top of the TV since."

It's unlikely that Jake will ever know the full story behind the intriguing events involving one solitary figurine in his temporary home.

Craig now lives in Calgary but his experience with a ghost took place in North Vancouver. The encounter occurred in the early 1990s in a setting almost created for a ghost story, for, yes, it was a dark and—well, if not stormy at least rainy—night. Craig was heading home, just before 11:00 p.m.

"I was just walking past one of the cemeteries in North Vancouver, not paying much attention to the traffic or anything like that," Craig recalled. "I was alone," he stated before adding dramatically, "as far as I knew."

Craig was about to find out that he was not, in fact, alone, even though he couldn't see whoever or whatever soon proved to be with him. "As I stepped [off the curb] to cross the street at the corner of the cemetery, I was grabbed by my left arm and literally turned around. I realized that a car had just come off the [cross] street and turned the corner. If I had stepped out, I would have been hit by the car."

After taking a second to recover from the shocks he'd just experienced, first of being grabbed and then realizing how narrowly he'd missed being involved in a possibly fatal accident, Craig turned to thank his rescuer. "There was nobody there when I turned around—literally no one," Craig remembered.

Not surprisingly, the young man hurried home. "When I got back to my apartment I took my shirt off. I had a distinctive handprint just above my elbow on my arm from where someone had grabbed me and pulled me. Even today I have goosebumps up and down my arms when I think of it."

To this day, Craig wonders if his walking beside a graveyard had anything to do with his ghostly guardian suddenly springing into action. "Could it have been somebody in the cemetery just watching [people] and seeing somebody not paying attention and realizing 'oh, he's going to get hit'?"

Craig's question was obviously rhetorical but he did reconfirm that there was nothing, visible, near him when the lifesaving intervention was made. He readily acknowledged, "It left me shaken for days after."

The caller with the following story began by describing the location of the haunted house as being "on the 700 block on 11th" in Brandon, Manitoba. It was a three-bedroom, two-storey house. The gentleman's two daughters, ages nine and twelve, slept in one of the upstairs bedrooms.

"Periodically, they would wake up at 2:00, 3:00 or 4:00 in the morning and see somebody standing at their bedroom door. This activity happened half a dozen times. The girls were startled. He just stood in the doorway so they took to closing their bedroom door. That helped," he recalled.

The man's daughters were not the only ones to be made aware of the presence in the house. "A while later my wife heard somebody walking up the stairway. It was an old house and the stairs creaked [when someone was on them]. The sound got to the top of the stairs but there was nothing. She never woke me up because she thought maybe it was the dog, but the dog was lying beside the bed on the floor.

"We moved out of the house about two years ago now. We just moved next door and I rented the old house to a young lady, her brother and her boyfriend. They had strange happenings that had never happened to us," the man acknowledged. "Somebody was turning off the washing machine and opening the lid on [it]. Late one afternoon the lady's boyfriend was having a snooze on the chesterfield and he felt somebody sit beside him. The cushion on the chesterfield sank as if somebody was sitting beside him. He thought it was the dog. He looked up and there was nobody there. He was deathly afraid.

"A few days after that the dog was in the house and made a beeline for the front door just as if somebody was breaking in and it [the dog] was going to tear the [intruder's] leg off. But, there was no one at the door." Many students of the paranormal believe that animals are far more sensitive to those beyond the confines of our own world, and it's quite likely that the dog sensed a threat that his owners weren't able to perceive.

Whether it was related to the hauntings or not, those tenants moved out of the house. The homeowner found new tenants and went about preparing the house for its next occupants.

"I had to go in and do some minor repairs. It was 10:00 or 11:00 at night and I could feel somebody in the house. I knew somebody was there. I was feeling kind of homesick for the old place. We'd lived there for twenty-seven years. I started talking to it, I said, 'Old house, don't worry, you're not going to be alone for long. There's a couple moving in with two little kids,'" the caller related.

The words were no sooner out of his mouth than he "felt an absolute cold chill."

The spirit may have been trying to communicate with him, because as soon as the new tenants moved in, the ghost seemed quite content. As a matter of fact, the caller reported, "Nothing has ever happened."

Curious as to who their invisible companion for all those years may have been, the caller told us that he'd done a title search on the property. The house was built in 1890, so it had certainly housed the dramas of many lives, but it was a couple who owned the place in the 1930s that the man felt was connected to the haunting.

"The fellow died in the house and willed it to his wife. It's possible that he's the ghost."

The caller might well be right but no matter who haunted the house, it's nice to think that he or she is enjoying its current earthly roommates.

This story also came through the phone lines, but in a slightly different way—it arrived on my computer via e-mail!

Patie's story began in 1988 when she and her husband Garry moved into the house they'd built in a suburb of Edmonton. Rather than being pleased with their new home, the woman acknowledged, "There was something about the house that I didn't like. I loved the yard, front and back, but the house itself, I hated it."

Patie didn't suspect, at first, that a ghost was involved.

It was only in retrospect that the young wife and mother recognized the first incident as possibly being paranormal in nature. Until then, she had been a skeptic who "never believed in ghosts"—never, that is, until she moved into a haunted house.

"My husband worked out of town during the week while I looked after our three small children, Chaantal, Shaala and Braden. About four to five months after we moved in, my wedding rings went missing. I usually placed my rings beside the phone shelf and one morning I noticed they were gone. I thought the kids had taken them [but] after searching every nook and cranny of the whole house—even the garbage—I came up with nothing," Patie explained.

When she wasn't able to find the rings, Patie filed a claim with her insurance company and had a new set of rings made. The only change she made was to have the three bands soldered together. Not long after, the young woman was "flabbergasted" to find the replacement rings missing.

"Where could they have possibly gone?" Patie wondered rhetorically. "I just couldn't figure it out. I wasn't about to get a third set made up and I never did find the rings."

Patie couldn't have known at the time that the disappearing rings were an eerie precursor of what was to come.

One of the first signs of a haunting can be apparent malfunctions in electrical fixtures or appliances. Such experiences were next for Patie, who explained, "As I was walking up the stairs to go to bed one night I turned off the hallway light behind me. I even turned around to make sure that all the lights were off—they were. For some reason, however, I woke up at 2:00 or 3:00 a.m. and noticed that the light in the hall going to the basement was on."

Thinking that there'd been a burglar, the young mother "put on [a] 'brave suit' and went downstairs and looked in every room. Everything was fine but, for the life of me, I could not figure out how the light came on."

The next day Patie checked the switch carefully and found nothing the matter with it. Perhaps the realization that she was dealing with something supernatural may have crept in, for she wrote, "This incident bothered me for a long time."

Children are often more sensitive to entities than adults are, which may have been the reason that Patie's eighteen-month-old son Braden was the next to be made aware of the ghost's presence. One evening, after the boy had been sleeping peacefully for some time, he suddenly began "screaming and crying," Patie related before adding, "I ran up the stairs. It looked like he was having a bad dream. I carried him downstairs to the kitchen. He was screaming and crying, 'Mommy, Mommy' as though he could not see me. His eyes were glassy. He was shaking and crying—crying uncontrollably. I got a cold wet cloth and dabbed his face as he was very red. Eventually he was okay [but] these dreams carried on and carried on for many days and even months after."

Remembering her concern, Patie continued, "Braden would tell me he had bad dreams but he couldn't explain what they were about and he would always cry when I asked him about them. They did not occur every day but maybe one or twice every two or three weeks for the next four or five months. Many times [after those night-mares] Braden couldn't see me even though I was holding him and trying to console him. He kept screaming my name and shaking. His eyes would be following 'something' around the room. It was very nerve-wracking. I felt so sorry for him every time this happened. I finally took him to my Baba's sister who performed some old Ukrainian ritual with blessed water, wax and a willow. He was okay for a while but then the dreams were happening again."

Sadly, whatever was disturbing Braden's sleep continued the entire time they lived in the house that Patie was coming to recognize as haunted.

Another incident occurred while Patie and the children were all watching television in a room that was separated from the kitchen by a railing. "We could see into the kitchen," she clarified. That was how they all happened to witness a cereal box move, apparently of its own volition, from the middle of the kitchen counter to the floor.

Patie acknowledged that it was then she "knew for sure that we weren't the only ones in the house."

Whatever was haunting the house must have had something of an obsession with tidy surfaces. When the children left orange peels on top of the roughed-in fireplace in the rumpus room, some hours later Patie watched as the rinds fell off the mantel "by themselves."

The ghost was clearly beginning to gain strength—enough to begin to manifest itself. Patie recalled, "One Sunday night I walked past the upstairs hallway and [out of] the corner of my eye I could have sworn I saw a sort of fog or mist about 4 feet [1.3 metres] high go into my bedroom."

Patie was alone in the house when she heard "what sounded like a board falling [and] scraping against the wall, [followed by the sound of] our closet door slamming real hard and loud footsteps. This all happened [directly] above me in our bedroom."

Yet again, the young woman summoned her courage and went to see what was wrong. She found nothing— nothing visible, that is.

One of the most predictable oddities about a haunted house is that it will be cold. There will either be random cold spots in certain rooms or the entire house will be abnormally cool. The latter was the case in Patie's new house.

"We had radiant floor heating. It was always so cold in our house. One day I even noticed frost in one corner of our kitchen about 6 inches [15 centimetres] up from the floor on the wall. My first impression was that the contractor built this house poorly ... I used to have the stove turned up high and the oven door open [in order for] me and the kids to stay warm in winter."

Presuming that the heating system had been installed incorrectly, Patie phoned the furnace company, "many, many, many times .... They came back time and time again and couldn't figure out why we weren't getting any heat as everything was hooked up correctly. I even threatened to call a local television station to report the heating company because they just weren't doing their job."

As with the missing rings, Patie did not connect the coldness of her home with the haunting—not until she read my books *Ghost Stories of Alberta* and *More Ghost Stories of Alberta*. She told me, "After reading some of the stories in your book it all came together for the first time. I realized it was the 'extra company' in our house that was making [it] so cold."

Also in true ghost story form, an animal was able to sense the presence in the house, even when the people were not. "There used to be a stray cat that would come in our house the odd time and was very friendly. One day Garry was home alone and the cat came to the deck window. Garry let it in. The cat was very friendly, purring, etc. Then a few minutes later, it just went berserk. This cat was trying desperately to get out of the house—running to every window to find a way out—Garry finally let it out, but he couldn't believe how crazy this cat got."

And all for no apparent reason.

Sadly, another trait of haunted houses, which I've documented in previous books, began to occur in Patie's home. "My husband and I weren't getting along after living in the house for four years." Finally, Patie moved out with the children. Garry stayed in the house but developed a chronic and progressive illness. "We are still very good friends and the kids and I visit him every two weeks or so, but it's interesting how his health failed and our marriage failed in that house."

"We sold the house a few months after our divorce. The realtor held an open house one Sunday. Only one person showed up and three weeks later that same person bought the house. That was quite strange but let me tell you, I was glad to get rid of it."

To this day Patie can't explain what went on during her family's four years in the house they had built. She did, however, "consult a psychic who told me that the spirit was an older man, in his 60s, who liked to play around with my son and have fun, but what I can't figure out is why—in a brand new house?"

Patie's and the children's lives are calmer now, but the episodes have left a lasting impression on the woman. "I know what I saw and went through and now I'm telling my story," she stated with conviction in her message to me. "After reading your book more of my questions were answered. I don't think about my experience much anymore but as I type this and think back I get the shivers. Many times when I drive [in the area] I wonder about our old house, how things are now. Then I just delete the thought out of my mind. I would rather not know."

As the following three stories demonstrate, not everyone labels the paranormal entity they encounter as a "ghost."

A woman who called Bill Turner's phone-in show on radio station CKLQ in Brandon shared some interesting insights and recollections about "forerunners"—paranormal beings or signals that indicate an event, most often a tragedy, is about to occur.

She began by acknowledging that her background included belief in the supernatural. "My mother's a great believer. She hates it when a bird comes to the window. She thinks it's bringing bad news."

Nevertheless, it was the image of a horse that the woman's mother recalled from childhood. "My grandfather loved horses. One night he was very ill and the horses were going crazy out in the corral. My mother and her sisters and brothers went to the window to [see what was causing the disturbance]. They could see a white horse out there. It was spooking their own horses. They didn't have a white horse nor did anybody around for miles. My grandfather died at that time. The white horse had come to take him."

The caller had also had a profound paranormal experience when she was only three years old. "I remember this so distinctly. I was lying in the crib sick with influenza. My younger sister was sick too. I was in another room but I could see across into her bedroom. I saw this dark thing come down the window and then go back up. That's when she died. It must have been death coming to take her but I didn't know it at the time."

The caller then went on to explain that the experience of forerunners in her life has continued into adulthood but their manifestation is different now. "For me it's a knocking. I've had several of these [incidences]."

She related a recent experience with phantom knocking sounds foretelling tragedy. Beginning in the week between Christmas and New Year's the caller remembered that she "could hear this knocking, every day. It was as if there was a woodpecker around or something but there was nothing."

The psychic messages continued until, "On Saturday, January 8 it [sounded] like I had a cup in the microwave oven and it was rocking. It was like knock, knock, knock. A pot on the stove will do that too but this seemed to be coming from the direction of the microwave. Then about 4:00 in the afternoon, it quit, completely quit. At 11:00 that night I got a call that my nephew had been killed at 4:00 that afternoon."

There was a moment of complete silence on the telephone lines and radio waves that linked the three of us—Bill Turner, the woman with the strange auditory experiences and I. Seconds later she continued, "This has happened several times. It scares me [because] after I hear this knocking, in a day or so I'll hear of someone's death."

By way of a conclusion, the woman told us about a friend of hers who believes that woodpeckers around her home foretell tragedy. "I think she's associating the birds with the bad news but really it's just the knocking." She might well be correct.

From what Lloyd, a caller to a CBC Radio phone-in show told us, there wasn't much question that he lived in a haunted house. Everyone who encountered the supernatural beings in his basement perceived them as an unpleasant odour, but individual descriptions of that odour varied considerably.

"We believe we have ghosts in the basement, a couple of them. They come and go. They haven't been around for quite some time now but [when they are] they're in the basement."

Lloyd related that the ghosts manifest as "a smell, a musty-type smell in 'pools' [of air] that move around in one section of the basement. This is not a nice-smelling thing. They're circular, about 2 or 3 feet [about 1 metre] in diameter. There's no consistency to when they show up or go away."

The man had checked the house thoroughly to rule out possible physical causes for the strange smells. "There's nothing there. We have been through it over and over again. There are no sewers, there's no water, there are no pipelines."

The inconsistent nature of this haunting makes it even more puzzling. "It comes and goes. One time there were two, one by the door and the other over by the closet. They were distinctively there. You could walk through them and smell them as you walked. Then you'd go out of them and then an hour or two later they'd be gone."

Lloyd and his family were certainly not the only ones to be aware of the basement-dwelling presences in his home. "Other people do notice it. When we have company that's usually when it comes out. I think of it as a musty smell, some people say rotten eggs, some people say it's a fishy smell."

And so, it would seem that something inexplicable is going on in this otherwise ordinary family home but each person who experiences it perceives it slightly differently.

Kenneth confessed right from the start of his call that he would have difficulty relating his experiences to us. "It will give me the 'geebers' to tell you this. Let me just start by saying this is a true story and that I remember it as clear as the day it happened. I was five years old."

The caller, his mother and his sister were staying overnight at a friend's house. Sleeping accommodations were makeshift, and Kenneth's mother made him a bed on the floor. The woman then tucked her daughter in the bed beside her.

"I woke up in the middle of the night," Kenneth recalled, stressing, "I know I was awake. I know when I'm awake and when I'm sleeping."

Unsure for a moment what had wakened him, the child looked around the room. "There was my mother standing in the doorway wearing a pair of jean shorts and one of those old tube tops that they had in the 1970s. I got up and walked right over to her. I touched her hand—it was real. I said 'Mom, what are you doing?' and this lady, it wasn't my mom but it looked like her, she said to me in this really whispery voice 'Go back to bed.'"

The man who was that little boy went on, "I felt very calm about it. I looked at the bed, and my mother and my sister were still lying on it. I turned around and my mother was standing in the doorway. For some reason I didn't freak out, I don't know why. I felt really calm. I just went back to bed and the next morning I asked my mom, I said 'Why were you standing in the doorway' and she said 'Oh, I wasn't standing in the doorway.' I remember that very clearly. That's a true story."

When pressed for details, Kenneth was able to supply them. The clothing that the apparition was wearing, for instance, "was an outfit my mother owned. I've seen it in pictures now that I'm older. Maybe she was having some kind of out of body experience that I witnessed but I touched it. It was her, I know my mother when I see her but it wasn't my mother because she was still in bed in her nightgown."

At that point Kenneth hesitated. Was he at the end of his story about his mother's doppelganger, I wondered. Not quite, apparently.

"In Saskatoon about three years ago I had a similar experience. I woke up and it was really foggy in the room. There was a presence and it said the exact same thing to me (in the same whispery voice). It said, 'Go back to bed.'"

This time, there was no question in Kenneth's mind: "It wasn't my mother, it was someone else. I don't know if what

I saw as a kid I just [perceived] as my mother because that was what I was used to."

Kenneth may never know the answer to his ponderings about the supernatural events in his life. His interpretation of perceiving the same entity differently as an adult than as a child shows great insight. It also supported the theory that, although our perceptions of it may vary, there is something out there that we can't fully comprehend.

When I'm doing radio shows, especially, I like to remind the hosts that radio stations are often haunted, which inevitably brings a shiver to the on-air personality. As a tribute to that theme, let's end this section of the book with the story of the ghost in the old CBC building at 90 Sumach Street in Toronto.

This commercial space was built in 1956, evidently long enough ago to become haunted. The ghost restricted itself to the fourth floor where its tall slender figure, dressed completely in black, was frequently seen at the elevator. Those who watched the phantom move said that, although they could not see anything in its arms, the apparition moved in a "jerky" manner as though its gait had been thrown off slightly by carrying a heavy load.

The Canadian Broadcasting Corporation centralized its Toronto operations in 1992 by moving to a large, new building. We can only hope that the tenants following CBC in that haunted building on Sumach Street have been enjoying their resident spectre as much as the employees at Mother Corp always did.

CHAPTER 4

The Spirit's Inn

Hotels serve as temporary homes and, as such, many are haunted. Some ghosts are permanent residents in Canadian hostelries. Other hauntings, as in some of the following stories, are more transient.

The Algonquin Hotel

The stately Canadian Pacific Hotels are as Canadian as the maple leaf and almost as important to many Canadians. The Algonquin Hotel in New Brunswick's historic St. Andrews-by-the-Sea is such a significant part of the tourist town that *The Canadian Encyclopedia* actually refers to them together, describing the heritage inn as "outstanding." When the hotel was built in 1889 (by a consortium of wealthy Americans), area brochures extolled the health benefits inherent in a vacation by the sea. "No hay fever here," prospective travellers were advised.

Advertising put out by the hotel itself described the seaside inn as "an incomparable resting place and retreat from the cares of business and the heat and dust and bustle of the city." That early advertising succeeded in attracting, among others, Canada's first prime minister, Sir John A. Macdonald, and his wife, Lady Macdonald.

Of course, such a hotel requires a large and dedicated staff. Christine James, now a school teacher in Owen Sound, Ontario, was just a youngster in 1966 when she enjoyed a summer as an employee of the popular tourist destination. During her stay, she had many memorable moments—one with a ghost.

Christine remembered the encounter this way: "I was working at the Algonquin Hotel in St. Andrews-by-the-Sea and rooming in a dorm with five other girls. The hotel is very old and so were the dorms. We each had a bed and dresser ... lined up three on each side of a large room. One night in late July, I was awakened by something at about

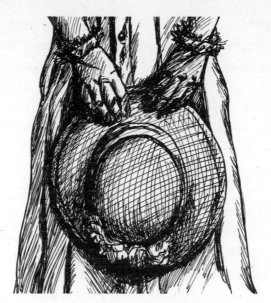

A well-dressed stranger from another time appeals for help.

2:00 a.m. Looking toward the doorway where the light from the hallway spilled into the far end of the room, I saw a shape moving toward my bed."

At this point in Christine's note, I fully expected her to make a reference to being afraid or, at the very least, startled by what she saw, but I was wrong.

Christine went on to relate the details of what she'd seen. "It was a woman in a dress about mid-calf, a summery dress, out of style for the times. She was wearing gloves and a hat."

Convinced that someone, probably a hotel guest, had lost her way, the girl called out to the image. "'Hello,' I said, but she didn't answer. In my mind, she needed some help or information of some kind and so I asked, 'Can I help you?' She still didn't answer. I felt no fear of any kind but was simply concerned for her because of the need I felt emanating from her."

Christine continued, "After I spoke to her the second time, quite a bit louder, one of the other girls was awakened and asked, 'What is it, Chris?' with a little irritation in her voice."

The sound of an additional human voice was apparently too much for the ghostly dorm visitor, for "the figure immediately disappeared."

Not knowing what else to do, Christine "rolled over and went back to sleep. The next day I was asked by my friend what had wakened me in the night. I tried to explain but realized right away that my answer seemed odd. Afraid of being accused of being 'crazy,' I just gave some vague explanation about a strange sound. Then [I] buried the incident deep in my memory and didn't mention it for many years. The strangeness of the conviction I had, that there was a somewhat old-fashioned person in need in our room that night, never left me, however."

It wasn't until years later, after reading a book (*The Ghost of Flight 401*, by John G. Fuller) about ghosts appearing in a certain type of airplane, that Christine James realized she'd had a supernatural encounter. Or, as Christine herself so poignantly put it, "What I had seen was a ghost. The sense that this person was in need and the total lack of fear were the two clues."

It is likely that this brief paranormal interlude was a temporal anomaly, the energy of a spirit reaching out across time. Sadly, we can never know whether or not, in life or in death, the ghost found the help she was seeking. But her presence that night in the mid-1960s left one young woman with an experience she'll never forget.

Pub "Creepy" Crawlers

As strange as it may seem, the province of Alberta has at least two extraordinarily popular pubs that were formerly funeral homes. What seems even stranger is that only one of them has a haunted Happy Hour. (The owners of the other establishment kindly offered to make up stories if I wished them to—no doubt entertaining but certainly not relevant here!)

Fortunately, for our purposes and for lovers of true ghost stories everywhere, the funeral-home-turned-pub that is haunted does have some wonderful paranormal tales associated with it. It is truly a place where the past and the present entwine. Not surprisingly, there's more than just one ghost in the place.

Twice, late at night, when Jean, one of the owners, was tidying up at closing, a "grey mist" formed just off the floor. Jean felt no fear but, amazingly, knew immediately that the presence was female and also that she was a friendly spirit who meant no harm.

The case was definitely different when Jean was working at her computer. "This one was frightening. It was right behind me. I looked, but there was nothing there. Then I looked back at the computer screen, and I could see a shadow."

Paralyzed by fear, the woman could only sit in front of the monitor as she became colder and colder. Before it finally left, this ghastly presence actually touched her. The terrified woman reported that the icy touch chilled her to the bone for the next two days.

An amusing anecdote from the pub's "other side" involves a cook whom the establishment's owners describe as "a tough guy." Despite his hardened demeanour, the man was badly shaken when a pair of women's red shoes and the hem of a red dress materialized out of nowhere before disappearing just as mysteriously.

As is the case with many haunted buildings, electrical and electronic appliances malfunction regularly and for no apparent reason. The sound on the bar's television set can range from mute to "blaring" in a matter of seconds, according to witnesses. The jukebox will occasionally emit a crackling sound that shouldn't exist. Repair people have been called in to investigate, but they've never been able to find any reason for the audio problems.

One morning, the entire building—from the basement to the roof—echoed with the sounds of phantom footfalls. Despite intense efforts to track down a possible intruder, no source for the noises was ever found.

Perhaps the strangest phantom sound, though, did not (seemingly) originate inside the building but (impossibly) came from out on the street in front of it. In the wee hours of a bitterly cold winter's night, with snow-covered streets and a thermometer reading of –30° C [–22° F], employees listened in disbelief to the distinct sound of a motorcycle tearing along the avenue. Of course, such a thing was not only ridiculous, but impossible—in this realm. It is possible, however, that what was heard was the last ride of a biker who had gone before and whose body had perhaps been brought to the funeral home after a fatal accident.

That speed-loving entity might also be responsible for at least one or two of the phantom smells that are sometimes detected in what used to be the embalming room. Jean works in that area frequently, and she's almost used to the sensations caused by the various and fleeting phantom smells that can pervade the room for varying lengths of time.

Customers, of course, are usually too distracted while they are enjoying the warm hospitality of the haunted hostelry, but at least one customer felt the ethereal spirits and found it necessary to leave long before having had a chance to even sip on the liquid spirits.

Jean is both philosophical and accepting of the unusual situation in this place of business. In conclusion, she simply commented, "I'm convinced the place is haunted. There are just too many things that happen."

So, next time you go out for a quick bite to eat, perhaps down to your neighbourhood tavern, it might be fitting to hoist a brew to those who have gone before—and may well still be there, in some form or another.

Spectral Speaker

Haunted bars and night clubs are probably a lot more common than the patrons to these establishments might like to acknowledge. One on East Pender Street in downtown Vancouver is an excellent example.

This particular bar had been in business for about twenty years before the building it was in was torn down, and it had been haunted for more than half its existence—ever since the establishment's owner died on the premises. It was always generally accepted that it was his spirit that the staff regularly detected.

The ghost was heard speaking on many occasions and, even when he was not heard, the staff could always tell when the entity was present. Serving dishes and kitchen utensils would shake and bang against each other, making not only a supernatural sight but an unearthly amount of noise.

This phantom, like many others, liked to play with electrical appliances. The industrial floor polisher was one of his favourite toys. When all else was quiet, the ghost would cause the polisher to turn on. As soon as the employees reacted with fright, he turned the machine off. Even then, the workers were not easily settled, for they reported hearing gales of ghostly laughter immediately after this stunt.

Only a very small piece of the ghost was ever seen, but that sighting was very officially documented—with the City of Vancouver police department. The incident took place one night as the manager was tallying up the night's receipts. As he worked, a movement caught his eye. The

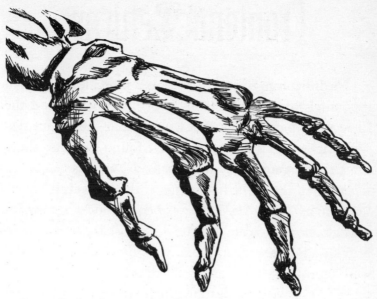

Police need a hand to solve this mystery.

man looked up to see a disembodied hand floating through the air. Although previously a skeptic about the stories he'd heard of the resident ghost, the man readily admitted to "being a little nervous" and certainly wasted no time in getting himself to the nearest police station. An officer accompanied him back into the building, but despite a thorough search, neither the hand nor any other part of the ghost was ever seen again.

Frontenac Returns

It's difficult to imagine two hotels more different than the Hotel Roosevelt in Hollywood, California, and the Château Frontenac in Quebec City. Despite their many dissimilarities, my investigations have found that they share some eerie, paranormal qualities.

An account of the hauntings at the Roosevelt can be found in my book *Ghost Stories of Hollywood*. For now, it's enough just to indicate that the posh hostelry continues to provide a home to people, many of them celebrities, who were significant to the area's development—even though those folks have been dead for many years. Ghosts within the Roosevelt either weren't known or weren't recognized until massive renovations to the hotel began. This situation is not too surprising: some sort of connection between the remodelling process and hauntings definitely seems to exist.

The stately old Château Frontenac was named after the man who was governor of New France for nearly twenty years in the 1600s. The ghost story at the luxurious Quebec City hotel follows much along the same lines as tales from the California hotel with one difference—the Quebec haunting was only temporary.

Nancy Murray, of the Château's administration, explained that "in 1993, during the hundredth anniversary, there were rumours that the place was haunted by Frontenac. He was a very benign spirit who was active only during that time." It was assumed that his spirit had come back to oversee the renovations.

The Château Frontenac: if you renovate it, he will come.

The Château Frontenac, perched high above the St. Lawrence River, has been a Canadian landmark ever since it opened on December 20, 1893. The hotel's marketing department explains that, even then, the luxurious accommodations were nothing short of remarkable. According to hotel brochures there were "170 rooms, including three magnificent suites while 93 rooms had a fireplace and a bathroom." These were truly "rare luxuries at the time." If he'd somehow been aware of the splendid hotel and that it was being named in his honour, the long-deceased governor might have been flattered. Today, the hotel is even more impressive, with 613 rooms, a swimming pool and an exercise room with state-of-the-art equipment. The castle-like hotel is an appealing combination of the best of the present and the past. And part of that past may be the lingering essence of Frontenac himself. If his ghost does wander the charming old place, it does so in his own time and place for, as Nancy Murray explained, "The last time he was spotted was [during the 1993 renovations] in the ballroom."

Ghost Attends Conference

Not all hotel hauntings are made by those who are long-deceased or even those who have been strongly associated with a place.

In 1961, Pierrette Champoux, then a well-known journalist, was attending a trade show at the Queen Elizabeth Hotel in her hometown of Montreal. As she was leaving the table after lunch on the Saturday session of the conference, Mademoiselle Champoux was delighted to run into an old friend, Emile Hamel, a fellow journalist. The two had been friends for nearly twenty years. Because of this close bond, Champoux had presumed that, if Hamel had made plans to be at the conference, he would've let her know some days before.

Perhaps because they felt awkward about a lack of recent communication with one another, neither he nor she mentioned that his presence was a surprise. They chatted happily about inconsequential matters for nearly half an hour before parting. As they said their goodbyes, Emile squeezed Pierrette's arm affectionately. She later recalled that, as they were bidding one another farewell, it crossed her mind that Emile wanted to add something to the conversation. She sensed that he'd been ready to introduce a new topic for discussion, perhaps an important matter, but had changed his mind because they were rushed for time.

Buoyed by her unexpected meeting, Pierrette Champoux moved along to the next obligation she had at the hotel. It wasn't until two days later that she learned of her friend

Emile Hamel's death—six hours before her conversation with him. Champoux's sense that her friend had wanted to tell her something important had certainly been correct. He no doubt wanted to tell her that he wouldn't be seeing her ever again. He had come back from beyond to say one last goodbye.

"Maud" Stays Home

A much more enduring hotel haunting can be found in a community on the shores of Lac des Deux Montagnes, just west of Montreal. The inn is not like the large, stately Château Frontenac or the Queen Elizabeth Hotel. This resort is smaller and was built as a private home. The ghost story traces back to those early days.

The resident phantom has, incorrectly, been called "Maud" for many years. Research indicates that, in life, the ghost was probably Mary Kirbride. Mary was a servant in the large home during the turbulent days of the 1837 Rebellion. Patriote Francois-Xavier Desjardines owned the house and was, therefore, Mary's employer. Mary felt no sympathy for the Patriotes and decided to tell that to Desjardines in no uncertain terms. Her decision proved fatal. Legend has it that he murdered her and, to get away with murder, buried her remains in the basement of his house.

Mary Kirbride, or Maud, has haunted the building ever since. She likes to draw attention to her presence by creating a distinctive and pleasant scent, knocking furniture over, slamming doors, singing and creating strange and inexplicable piles of rocks near a particular door. Mary's eeriest manifestation takes the form of a crop of mushrooms that grows in the inn's basement—a crop confined to only one small area, the area where the murdered woman is buried.

Haunted Landmark Razed

On Wednesday, July 19, 2000, a long-standing, but no longer proud or active, Alberta institution came crashing down. The Bruin Inn had been a landmark at the corner of St. Anne and Perron Streets for as long as anyone could remember. Not surprisingly, everyone in and around the city of St. Albert had an opinion about the hotel.

What is surprising is that the place, at least once, became the topic of a discussion that took place halfway around the world. This international story involves an American soldier serving in Saigon during the Vietnam War, who struck up a conversation with a Canadian reporter also stationed there. The serviceman asked if the scribe knew about a popular watering hole just outside Edmonton.

"It's called the Grizzly or the Brown," the serviceman explained. The Canadian, who was actually from southern Ontario but had trained in Edmonton, responded, "Are you talking about the Bruin?" From that tenuous link made so many thousands of kilometres away, a friendship was

It was last call for two resident ghosts when the Bruin Inn was demolished.

forged, just one of the many friendships made possible by the Bruin Inn connection, but surely the one formed farthest away from the pub itself.

Although we know exactly when this famous (some would say infamous), empty and by then ugly building's existence ended, pinning a date on its conception is a little more difficult: there had been drinking establishments at that location since at least 1885. It's generally accepted, though, that the first incarnation of the hotel named the Bruin Inn was constructed in 1929. Its California Mission-style architecture made it the talk of the era. The building may have been cutting-edge in design, but, by definition, was oddly out of place in north-central Alberta.

The Bruin Inn's early days were anchored in simpler times. Prohibition laws had just been overturned, finally freeing Albertans to quaff an alcoholic beverage legally, and the destructive momentum of what became known as the

Great Depression was only just beginning. It was in this setting that lawmakers saw a potential problem brewing. It seemed that then, as now, when drinking alcohol, some men tended to start fights and these altercations often began as disputes over the perceived or real attentions of a woman. Fortunately, those in positions of authority were confident that they had the answer to the problem. Men and women must not drink together—men must drink in one room and women in another. And, as if this proposal was not completely ridiculous enough as it stood, the ruling was made effective only in the cities of Calgary and Edmonton. Away from the confines of those two metropolises, men, even when drinking, could apparently be counted upon to act as gentlemen when women were around. Many ramifications flowed from the institution of this sex-segregation decree, but the most important one for the Bruin Inn was that, owing to its proximity to Edmonton, it became a popular and profitable business endeavour attracting many Edmonton couples who, understandably, wished to share an alcoholic beverage while in the same room.

It is likely that it was during this era that the Bruin Inn first became haunted. The female phantom resident was regularly seen walking along the upstairs hallway of the inn. Inevitably, as she made her ghostly rounds, the misty figure would pass by the windows overlooking St. Anne Street, much to the amazement of passersby. No one has ever suggested who the spirit might have been or what her connection with the Bruin Inn was when she was alive, but neither has anyone who ever observed the spectre questioned its authenticity.

The second paranormal presence reputed to reside in the old place is the spirit of an older man. A little more is known about this soul. It is said that he died in the bar while listening to a story being told by a fellow drinker. Legend has it that, when the story-teller came to the punch line of his anecdote, he slapped his hand down on the table for emphasis. The elderly chap was so startled by the sudden action that he suffered a fatal heart attack. Donald Watkins, Ph.D., who wrote a paper entitled "The Scourge of Fire," speculates that this man may in his afterlife have been the ghost who was frequently seen in the guest rooms located directly above the hotel's front doors.

During the three years prior to its demolition, the Bruin stood vacant. It's likely that both apparitions remained happily in residence for that time because at least one theory holds that ghosts prefer and even flourish in empty buildings. Many anecdotal reports seem to support this notion. If it is true in the case of the haunted and abandoned building in downtown St. Albert, then the arrival of the demolition squad at the corner of St. Anne and Perron Streets on that fateful Wednesday in July 2000 must have been the saddest surprise of the resident phantoms' afterlives.

Spirits at the Bar

Jim Lawrence struck me as having a strong entrepre-
neurial streak—not as someone likely to be involved in
paranormal stories. But, even to the most pragmatic individuals, if ghosts are evident, it doesn't make much sense
to try to dismiss them as imaginary.

Jim began his account by writing a sentence guaranteed
to capture my attention: "My personal relationship with the
bar began in 1972, but other people have related experiences that go back a lot further."

He continued, "When we moved to our old farm in
Quebec, I went into partnership with another fellow in a
bar located next door. I lived there [on the property] full
time [so it was agreed that] I would manage the bar and we
both worked it on weekends. It was inside a 125-year-old
farm house that had been extensively renovated."

Having provided that background, Jim launched into the
chilling evidence that the place was heavily haunted. "One
morning, my wife (Eve) and I were at the bar cleaning up
when we both heard someone walking along the upstairs
hallway. Since I knew we were alone in the bar, I called my
dog, a large male Labrador retriever who was sleeping in a
corner, and we headed upstairs to see who the intruder was.
Someone could have come in the front door without our seeing him or her. When we got to the landing (one short flight
up, in front of another short flight, leading to the hallway)
the dog refused to go any farther. His hair raised on his back
and he started to growl. Suddenly he yelped and turned and
ran back down the stairs."

The dog's behaviour surprised Jim. "I thought he was afraid of a prowler, so I continued up the stairs and searched the entire second floor. There was nobody there."

The Lawrences tried to put the strange occurrence out of their minds and, for the most part, were successful. It wasn't until "later that year, at Christmas" that the issue resurfaced.

"My mother-in-law and my wife's sister stayed overnight in the bar on the second floor in one of the two bedrooms. Next morning when [I] asked how they slept they were angry with me for not telling them someone else was there too. 'We heard him walking up and down the hallway outside our door all night,'" Jim's relatives explained with evident annoyance.

Not surprisingly, the man's explanation that there had been no one else in the building did nothing to ease his guests' concerns, but he tried to carry on as though there was nothing out of the ordinary. It was fully two years later before the family had any external confirmation that theirs was a supernatural piece of real estate, for that was when the previous owner of the property dropped in unexpectedly.

"I was fiddling around with something at the time. He introduced himself and told me he used to own the farm on which the bar was situated and that he had lived in the building. I invited him in for a tour of the renovations. After a cup of coffee, he left. As he was getting into his car, he stopped and asked me, 'Do you still have the ghost that walks up and down the hall at night?'"

Jim still had no explanation for the haunting, but at least he knew there was nothing inherently dangerous about the situation. After all, it had been going on, unchanged, for many years.

CHAPTER 5

Historically Haunted

Canada does not have a long period of recorded history, especially when compared to other countries. However, certain historical events that occurred in Canada have given us a sprinkling of supernatural stories.

Ghost Brothers

The following is a fascinating tale that I first heard in September 1998 on an airplane flight from my home in Edmonton to Toronto. I was on my way to do some book promotion and to visit family, so I was not thinking of ghost story collecting at all. Even so, a stroke of good luck, or some other positive force, was at work for me. My seat-mate for the trip not only was a fascinating person, but she had an intriguing story to tell. I listened with rapt attention and then, later that night, scribbled down as many of the woman's words as I could recall. Sadly, some of the details had already escaped my memory but, as there wouldn't have been enough time available to have that story included in my *Ontario Ghost Stories* book, I wasn't as concerned as I might have been.

Fortunately, more as a courtesy than anything else, I had given my travelling companion one of my business cards. In January 2000, I was delighted to receive a letter from her describing her family's ghost story even more precisely than she had as we flew together over thousands of kilometres of Canadian landscape.

Ruth Drummond lives in Sundridge, Ontario, a community just west of the western boundary of Algonquin Park. She began relaying her intriguing tale this way: "My father's two younger brothers, my Uncle Edwin and Uncle Russell, enlisted in the Canadian Army in 1916. Uncle Edwin was killed in the spring of 1918 and was buried in France. Uncle Russell was listed as missing, presumed killed in action, just a few days before the Armistice in November 1918.

"Grandma and Grandpa Willan [Edwin and Russell's parents] had pictures of the boys set in those beautiful oval frames with convex glass that were popular at the time. When Mother and Dad took over the family farm, the pictures remained in the parlour under their care. I was raised with the pictures of these treasured uncles. I found them fascinating, with the hint of impish mischief that played at the corners of each mouth, and eyes that followed you no matter where you were in the room—a feature typical of pictures in the early 1900s.

"Eventually, Mother and Dad sold the farm and moved to a new home. The pictures went with them, again hung in a corner, facing each other, as they had always been. In 1978, after Dad's death, when Mother could no longer remain by herself in her home, there was a question of who would take care of [the photographs of] Uncle Edwin and Uncle Russell. They ended up with Leonard Willan, my brother's son, and his wife, Trudy. Trudy, who treasures family history, proudly hung the pictures side-by-side in their living room.

"In 1991, when Trudy and Leonard were visiting us in Sundridge, Trudy asked me if I believed in ghosts. When I hesitantly said, 'Yes,' she told me what had happened while the pictures hung in her home. [Up to that point] she had been reluctant to tell the story, even to other family members.

"Within a month after the pictures were hung in Leonard and Trudy's home, Leonard got up one morning and announced that the pictures had to go. 'Those two boys ran through the house all night,' he said. 'I didn't get any sleep.' After a few days, when [Leonard] was even more agitated and insistent, Trudy decided to move the pictures deep within their daughter Lynn's closet. No one knew where she had put them. The following morning, six-year-old Lynn complained at breakfast that she couldn't sleep all night because those two boys in army clothes made too much noise playing games and chasing each other around her bedroom. It was then that Trudy decided to pass the pictures back to her father-in-law, Gaines Willan. She did not tell him why she wasn't keeping the pictures."

Ruth continued, "Having no suitable spot to hang the pictures, Gaines tucked them into a cubbyhole under the eave in his home. Sometime later, Gaines's daughter Linda came home for a visit. She slept in the bedroom next to the hidden pictures. The next morning, she went to have coffee with Trudy and complained that she hadn't slept well because these two kids in army uniforms had chased each other through the upstairs all night. From then on, whenever Linda stayed overnight, she refused to sleep upstairs, choosing instead to curl up on the chesterfield.

"I then provided Trudy with some background about the uncles that she did not know. Uncle Edwin and Uncle Russell joined the Army when they were still kids, just seventeen years old. The two boys were almost like twins, just ten months apart in age, and usually inseparable. Tales of their pranks on each other and unsuspecting members of the community were often repeated and enjoyed by those who escaped their wit.

"In 1992, when my brother and his wife retired to Wheatley [on the shore of Lake Erie, south and east of Windsor, Ontario], again the question was, what do we do with Uncle Edwin and Uncle Russell? The family decided to donate the pictures to the Royal Canadian Legion in

Wheatley. The Legion members graciously accepted the gift and hung the [pictures of the] brothers, with an identifying bronze plaque, in the Legion Hall. Shortly after that, the Legion building mysteriously caught fire and was badly damaged by smoke and water. Did the displaced brothers have anything to do with it? Who knows?"

The pictures survived the fire and Ruth's family is once again in possession of them. "The photographs and glass are still in good condition but the wooden frames are warped and the finish is peeling. They are packed in [a] storage room, with other antiques, waiting to be restored."

Of late, there have been "no antics from the brothers."

Brother from Beyond

It was well into evening, having been dark outside for several hours. The workday had been long and demanding. John Sherbroke (occasionally spelled Sherbrooke) and George Wynyard, two young Army officers, gratefully settled themselves on chairs within the circle of warmth provided by a glowing hearth. Their regimental barracks at Sydney on Nova Scotia's Cape Breton Island were new and, if the accommodations could not be called luxurious, they were, at least for their time and purpose, comfortable. Both John, a captain at the time of the incident I am about to relate, and George, then a lieutenant, had endured considerably more spartan accommodations earlier during their military careers and probably would again. For now, the two were content to appreciate what they had—safety, shelter and some time to relax and enjoy an hour or so of recreational reading.

The officers knew their time to read would be limited. Soon the darkness of the night would overpower the lamp's flickering light, forcing them to abandon their novels in favour of their bedrolls. For the moment, the men were able to indulge themselves in a way not many of their era could. The date, you see, was October 15, 1785.

In the growing darkness, John and George put down their books. For a while, the men sat in companionable silence. Some moments later, John spoke.

"If we're going to stay up any longer, we'll need the fur wraps. This cold goes to a man's bones. It feels like midwinter does at home," he commented, referring to their British Isles heritage.

John hadn't really expected a reply from his colleague, but he was a bit surprised not to have his comments acknowledged. A quick glance toward George told him his friend had not heard a word he'd said. What's more, even considering the lack of light, it was obvious that George's usually ruddy complexion had lost all of its colouring. Some years later as John recounted the incident, he was quoted as saying, "I have often heard of a man being as pale as death, but I never saw a living face assume the appearance of a corpse as Wynyard's appeared at that moment. His face was pathetic. He was completely silent and somehow seemed emaciated."

Turning to follow the direction of his friend's rapt gaze, Sherbroke immediately understood what had mesmerized Wynyard. Impossibly, there was a figure of a man in the room. The spectre stood between the two men, staring at George with "a look of melancholy affection."

After uttering an oath, Wynyard spoke in a barely audible monotone, "That is my brother." Moments later, the phantom diffused and vaporized as mysteriously as it had formed. The sudden appearance, and then equally sudden disappearance, of the image stunned both men.

John broke the stillness by stating, "That can't have been your brother. He is assigned to a post in England."

At first, George could only nod in agreement. When he had recovered his wits, the young lieutenant wisely suggested that they search the premises and find the intruding prankster. They found no one, nor any trace that anyone but themselves had been in the room. The men were not surprised. The only door leading outside the building was in the room where they'd been sitting. It would have been impossible for anyone to have opened that door, much less gone through it, without their knowing.

Badly shaken by the experience, the men agreed to tell no one about it, but George did record the time, place and nature of the incident in his day book. He tried his best to put the occurrence out of his mind, but as each day passed he became more and more troubled. He became obsessed by the mystery and, before long, the men he worked with noted dramatic changes in their companion's appearance and personality. Eventually, John was forced to relate the details of the ghostly incident to the others in the regiment. Much to George's surprise, the men were sympathetic and supportive. They encouraged the man to write home to England and ask if there might be any news the family wished to share with him.

Winter and then spring passed without word from the Wynyard family. Given the era, the lack of reply surprised no one. Travel was slow and hazardous at best. The entrance to the port was jammed with ice for many months of the year. Information between the colonies and the homeland was not expected nor exchanged frequently. What was surprising was that, although it had been George Wynyard who had mailed a specific request for a reply, it was John Sherbroke who received the first letter. The note was from a mutual friend. He asked that John break some tragic news to George—his adored younger brother had died the previous October. A quick calculation of the time difference across the Atlantic Ocean confirmed that death had occurred at exactly the moment the young man's spectre had appeared, and then disappeared, thousands of kilometres away in the regimental barracks at Sydney on Cape Breton Island in Nova Scotia.

After a period of delayed mourning, George Wynyard was finally able to get on with his life and made a success of everything he did. Some might have said he was trying to live for two. He was knighted and became a colonial governor. He rarely mentioned seeing the ghost of his brother. When the incident was brought up for discussion by others, Wynyard always asked that the topic be dropped immediately. Seeing the ghost of his brother remained a profoundly painful moment in the man's life.

We can only hope that, on George Wynyard's death bed, the ghostly visitation of years before came full circle and that the spirit of the younger Wynyard appeared to guide his brother to the great beyond.

The Thing

"The Thing." That's what they called it in the mid-1930s when the town of Brooks, Alberta, was occasionally being haunted by a phantom light. The first newspaper report of the supernatural event hit the streets courtesy of the *Brooks Bulletin* on a cold Wednesday in January—January 10, 1934, to be precise. For inquiring minds who might have wondered but were afraid to ask, the headline writer boldly posed the front-page question, "Ghost Seen at Riverbow?"

It seems that "an eerie, sinister-looking light" had been observed "2 miles [about 3 kilometres] south" of the Brooks' post office on the evening of New Year's Day. Although the observer's name was not given, the Depression-era scribe assured his or her readers that "this person appeared to be in full possession of his faculties." This state of trustworthiness was verified when the reporter acknowledged that, "given all the parties being held at that time of year, seeing spirits was in most cases the consequence of other spirits imbibed during the night's festivities."

As word spread through the community that something out of the ordinary, perhaps otherworldly, was happening, another witness stepped forward. This man, identified only as Mr. Stone, was described as being one of the most respected members of the community. When he reported seeing the ghost light a few evenings after it had first been reported, he was a bit confused and uncertain about exactly what he had seen, which led him to ask if anyone knew "who or what might have been cavorting around outside, with a 'lantern or something.'"

When a third unnamed, but apparently equally reliable, member of the community saw the apparition, which had by then been described as "eerie, sinister-looking, resembling a great bloodshot eye,"a sort of vigilante committee was formed (perhaps the first team of Ghost Busters in Alberta?). Disappointingly, they reported, "all observations have proved fruitless."

Folks were beginning to get a handle on tracking The Thing. They noted that one of its most frightening characteristics was its ability to suddenly appear 30 yards (about 28 metres) away from the witness, "quiver for an instant, and then disappear."

The spectre apparently remained in the area the following week. A front page editorial in the *Brooks Bulletin* stressed that, in such modern and enlightened times, not to believe in the supernatural simply meant one was not fully aware of the burgeoning world around one. Although the editorial writer, a man named Percy H. Hill, was unsure of what to call the phenomenon that had been haunting the area—he offered the words "ghost," "disembodied spirit," "soul" and "apparition"—he did exhort readers to be aware that "there are scientific explanations based on the laws of light and sound which demonstrate quite clearly the conditions under which a psychic vision can be seen or a voice heard by anyone who happens to be around at the time."

Hill dismissed as fanciful fabrication "the clutching hand, death-dealing type of spook-story."

Those two reports of the Depression-era haunting at Brooks might have been all but forgotten if not for the tenacious and well-honed skills of Calgary's paranormal researcher W. Ritchie Benedict, who uncovered the archival stories and brought them to my attention.

Natalie Edwards, of Edmonton, alerted me to the ghost light in the Myrtle Creek area of Alberta as described in the book *The Myrtle Creek Story: A History of a Pioneer Rural School District*. Here writer Wilfred Krause describes a "mysterious light said to roam the creek valley and trails." Like the newspaper reporter in Brooks, Krause acknowledges that the phenomenon is not understood and is certainly frightening to some who see it—"especially if seen close to midnight," he added.

Even today, the appearance of a ghost light, sometimes called an earth light, a Will o' the Wisp, or by the Latin designation of *Ignis Fatuus*, is not understood. Of course, there are those who claim the eerie brightnesses are merely swamp gas and buttress their point by referring to sightings near prairie sloughs. Since ghost lights have also been documented on roads near the geographic centre of Vancouver Island, this attempt at a prairie-based explanation is difficult to accept.

Whether the lights occur naturally or supernaturally, perhaps even as a physical manifestation of a human soul, we do not know. What we do know is that, even today, a phenomenon once described as "The Thing" is proof that we live in a thought-provoking world with many misunderstood, and spooky, components to it.

Knock, Knock, Who's There?

Noel, Nova Scotia, is on the south shore of Cobequid Bay. This small community has been visited by phantom sounds—sounds that twice, some say, were harbingers of the two world wars.

Reta Laffin grew up in Noel. She remembers how, when she was a child, the eerie sounds captivated the local residents.

The personable lady recalled, "During the summer or early fall of 1938, a strange thing happened in East Noel. That was the year the Bone Knockers made their presence known. No one knows for certain just what a Bone Knocker is or even if a Bone Knocker is. The noise made by the so-called Bone Knockers resembled the noise of two dried bones being rattled together. This phenomenon stayed in East Noel for two or three weeks.

"Every night, the Point Road was lined with cars while the occupants stood outside and listened for the Bone Knockers. Men searched the surrounding ditches, swamps and marshes for the elusive noisemakers, but to no avail. The Bone Knockers knocked on. One minute, [their sound] was heard right nearby on your right side but, two seconds later, it was heard far off in the distance to your left .... Certainly, no two ever sounded at the same time."

Mrs. Laffin explained, "I remember I was ten or eleven years old when all of this was taking place. I was so very brave each night after supper when we started out for the Point Road to listen to this wondrous thing that had come to our small community. But, coming home was another story. I was scared to death coming home in the dark."

Some of the adults in the area had a bit more insight into the phenomenon than any of the children could have. "Local legend tells us that the Bone Knockers first came to East Noel at the time of the death of a particularly wicked school master. I never did hear what he did that was so wicked, nor do I know what year that happened. Rumour has it that, as his body lay in the parlour of the house [where he had lived and died], the house itself became over-run with chirping crickets and croaking frogs. When the school master was buried in the old cemetery at the old point, it is said that the crickets and frogs followed the market wagon bearing the casket and body all the way to the graveyard.

"Apparently [the pests] disappeared then, but the Bone Knockers were ... heard for the first time. [Then] they were apparently silent ... until 1913 when they again made their presence known.

"I remember [in 1938] one dear old lady in the community saying 'Oh dear, there's bound to be some great disaster. The last time the Bone Knockers were heard was just before the Great War.' World War II was declared in 1939."

To this day, no one has been able to explain the phantom sounds that temporarily haunted the Nova Scotia community. Thankfully, the eerie sounds that the residents credited to "Bone Knockers" have not been heard since and, we should all hope, they never will be heard again.

The Real McCoy?

Georgian Bay, in Ontario, forms the eastern portion of Lake Huron and is perhaps one of the most beautiful, rugged spots in all of Canada. Many islands dot the bay's waters and legend has it that at least one of those is haunted. Every year, at the September full moon, a gaggle of ghost hunters gather to hear a murdered man protest his death.

In life, the spirit was a man named McCoy. Although his first name has been lost in time, the McCoy Islands—"Little McCoy" and "Big McCoy"—were apparently named either in his honour or his dishonour. From all accounts, the real McCoy was a far from admirable fellow. Not only did he cheat and steal, he bragged about his abilities at both.

In death, he has become the sort of spectacular spectre from which nightmares are created. His spirit manifests annually as two heart-piercing shrieks echo through the island's forests and the waters of the surrounding bay. Approaching the island to listen for the ghostly howl has become a rite of passage for many area youths and, for others, a yearly ritual. To date, it is said, the auditory presence has not disappointed anyone. The ghoulish screams are still heard and have not lost their ability to terrify those who go to listen.

But Big McCoy Island may have been a home to spirits long before anyone of European descent set foot on the land. Many people believe that a symmetrical mound of stones at one of the island's small eastern bays is an ancient and sacred burial place.

Ghostly Chief

Just inland from Corner Brook, Newfoundland, lies the aptly named Grand Lake and, as anyone familiar with Newfoundland knows, Glover Island lies in the middle of Grand Lake. What isn't as well known is that, on certain October days, a piece of Glover Island's shoreline was haunted by the ghost of a long-deceased Beothuk chief.

The great native leader lived in the early 1800s. He was well respected by his people and European immigrants alike, trading frequently and always fairly. The last time the chief was seen at a favoured trading post, however, he refused to take any payment for the furs he had brought in with him.

"The Great Spirit has given me a sign. He'll be calling me soon and I no longer need anything the white man can give me," the elderly chief explained. The traders tried to persuade him to take payment, but the esteemed leader merely turned away from the counter and left the rough-hewn building.

Several days later, a European trapper, who had not been at the post when the chief last visited, reported seeing a very strange sight. "I saw the old chief, sitting in his canoe on the waters near the shore of the island. He had his arms crossed, his paddle was in his lap and he was gazing off into the distance. What was stranger still was that the chief's canoe was moving steadily down the lake, against the winds and tide. I called out to him to see if he needed any help, but he didn't seem to hear me," the man related.

Those who'd been in the post, and heard the chief's news that the Great Spirit would soon be calling him, nodded

Final voyage

quietly. "You might have seen the chief's last few moments on this earth. Perhaps he was just waiting to be summoned," they suggested to the puzzled man.

Those traders may well have been right, for the chief was never seen alive again. At first, everyone who knew the old man missed him, but then, over the years, his warm and welcome personality seemed to be forgotten. It was just then, when the memory of him began to fade, that his image began to appear on the island. The ghost was always seen sitting on a rock, his blanket wrapped around him.

When passersby called out to the apparition, he would turn his head toward them but, by the time they'd maneuvered their canoes nearer to the shore, the chief's ghost had vaporized. Those who saw his apparition over the years reported that the colours of the blanket he clutched about him were becoming more and more faded. By now, both the chief's ghost and his blanket have faded from sight completely.

Evil, Cursed, Haunted Or All Three?

Treasure hunters from any country are sure to know all about a tiny island in Nova Scotia's Mahone Bay said to contain a treasure. Some people are sure that the island was haunted long before the first attempt was made to unearth whatever may be buried there.

The generations-long mystery of Oak Island's "Money Pit" began in 1795. When or how it will end is anyone's guess, but some believe that the mystery will not be solved, and the treasure buried in the Money Pit not found, until the oak trees that once covered the island are completely gone and until seven men have died there.

Meanwhile, the futile search for buried treasure (which may or may not ever have existed) has desecrated the once-pristine island. A count of the number of ghosts on Oak Island, and even the timeline for the alleged hauntings, depends on whose line of investigation you follow.

Europeans settling in the area avoided Oak Island, preferring the nearbly island dotted with coniferous trees. Strange stories soon began being told about the place. Although a longstanding and widely accepted legend that pirate William Kidd had buried his treasure where oak trees were abundant may have helped to fuel these superstitious stories, the result was that, early on, Oak Island was labelled "evil."

Even though there was no human habitation on the island, the original settlers in the area often saw lights

Two hundred years, six dead men, one buried treasure?

dancing about in the oak forest. On certain nights, even voices could be heard emanating from the place. Some said that the brightness of the mysterious lights illuminated an extraordinary sight: men, dressed in clothes from a long-ago era, digging a hole in the ground on Oak Island—a hole big enough, perhaps, to bury a treasure chest. For those earliest observers, though, a more disturbing event occurred when two men who set out to explore Oak Island never returned.

Many people have devoted much of their lives to seeking the treasure they are certain lies just beyond, or below, their reach. A few of those obsessed searchers have paid for their intense curiosity and dogged determination about the eerie spot with their very lives.

The treasure hunt began officially in the late 18th century when Daniel McGinnis, a young settler to the area, visited the island. He noted a circular depression of land in a clearing and a scarred tree at the edge of the clearing.

It was obvious that those scars had not occurred naturally. It looked as though they had been caused when an oak branch had been used as a fulcrum for a pulley.

The sight was enticing: McGinnis, like all settlers in that area, knew that pirates often buried their treasure on the shores of the mainland as well as somewhere on the many islands scattered about the bays in the area. Thinking that he may have stumbled upon the location of a buried cache of riches, Daniel headed back home to enlist the help of two friends. The next day, filled with hope, those lads began digging, and hence began a process that is carried on, by others, to this day.

Those initial searchers, and the many who followed, discovered a pit consisting of sharply perpendicular walls and a descending series of oak reinforcing platforms. The existence of the pit certainly explains the slump in the land, and oak boards laid every 3 metres [10 feet] down explains the clearing itself, as the trees must have been chopped down to build the "shelves."

It was evident that a great deal of precise, painstaking and backbreaking work had been done and that whoever had dug this vertical tunnel wanted to hide something. By the early 1800s, treasure hunters had made their way nearly 30 metres (100 feet) straight down into the pit. There, much to their surprise, they discovered a rock unlike any other they'd ever seen in the area. Stranger still, it had an inscription in hieroglyphics unfamiliar to any of the hunters. The mystery might have been solved right then, but, as night had fallen, further work had to be postponed until the next morning. However, by the time morning dawned, it was too late to examine the stone more carefully. The pit had flooded. After failing to bail

Searchers continue to seek treasure like this.

out the first shaft, the workers tried to sink a parallel shaft. The second tunnel flooded, and they ran out of money.

By the middle of the 1800s, the hunt was on again. Even though the island is now littered with pits and tunnels, no treasure has been found. Rather than be discouraged, treasure hunters feel that history is on their side. After all—thanks to their obsessive explorations on Oak Island, the trees are "gone" and six men have died. The requirements of the curse have almost been met.

Today the treasure hunt has incorporated all the advantages of industrial and technological progress. Computers and heavy equipment are now enlisted in the work to uncover the riches.

Southern Ontario mining engineer Stephen Bartlett theorizes that the lights seen in the forest might actually have been a very good clue as to the location of the treasure.

"'Earth lights/ghost lights' are derived from earth faults, geology/geophysics. Caves and crevices are typical of faults, thus allowing [and possibly indicating] natural hiding places for treasure."

A bit of sensitivity or a close and careful examination of the tales told by pioneer searchers might have been better utilized. Despite the powerful curse that apparently exists to protect the treasure, many old-timers reported that, as they dug, they were visited by helpful paranormal entities. One group of prospectors looked up from their task to see a large rowboat approaching the island. The vision was clear—eight men in the boat, four per side, each at an oar. The scene was so real to the men working on the tunnel that one of them called out a greeting. In response, the vision simply disappeared as quickly as it had appeared.

Could the sighting have been a mass hallucination caused by overwork? Possibly, but it is also certain that those diggers shared the rare paranormal experience of retrocognition. For just a few minutes they were able to see an incident that had actually occurred many years before. Perhaps those were the ghosts of the men who had buried the very cache the searchers were after. We will never know whether the phantoms would have remained visible if the one man had not spoken. If they had remained visible, the temporal anomalies might have led them straight to the treasure.

Other ghosts on the island have been more aggressive about trying to help the treasure hunters. Dr. Helen Creighton's landmark research turned up first-hand stories from people who had had ghostly encounters on the island. In at least two cases—and it might have been the same ghost each time, because the message was the same—the treasure hunters were advised that they were not digging in the right place.

Even though over two hundred years, and at least as many tellings, have passed, descriptions of the ghosts are amazingly consistent and often have the spirits clad in red coats. During one winter, a child watched in awe as two men wearing red coats walked toward her. She ran to get her father, but he could find no trace of the presences—not even any tracks in the snow. A young boy out rowing was terrified when he too saw the ghosts dressed in red.

Other sightings have been less distinct but come with equally and decidedly paranormal qualities. In addition to the lights in the forest, people have seen pillars or shafts of light as well as strange, shadowy shapes. If these are not spectres themselves, such illusions are usually associated with hauntings.

At this writing, the ghost story of Oak Island has no conclusion. When, or if, the enigma is solved, the tiny island off the coast of Nova Scotia will be, at least briefly, internationally known to more than just treasure hunters and ghost lovers.

CHAPTER 6

They Came Back

Why the spirits of some people return to the earthly plane is a mystery as enticing as the phenomenon of ghosts itself. The following stories describe particularly dramatic incidents of souls that have come back for one reason or another.

Possession by a Poltergeist

When the movie *The Exorcist* was released in 1973, it had a powerful effect on people. Many who saw the movie were horrified and deeply disturbed by it. Because of this intense emotional reaction, moviegoers by the millions were drawn to see this innovative film, the story of a little girl possessed by an evil spirit.

Imagine how terrified the citizens of tiny Amherst, Nova Scotia, were when they had to deal with the reality of such a phenomenon—in 1878.

Summer was just giving way to autumn when a Methodist minister, Reverend A. Temple, began hearing strange reports about one of the families in his parish. At first, he could hardly believe the accounts being told. Surely these stories that Esther Cox, the teenage sister of Olive Teed, had become possessed by some unnatural force could not be true. Such a thing seemed impossible. Temple knew the family well. They were fine people.

Daniel Teed, Olive's husband, had a good job in the town's shoe factory. The Teed household included the couple's two young sons, Daniel's brother John, as well as Olive's unmarried siblings, William, Jane (or Jennie, as she was fondly called) and Esther Cox. All were God-fearing folk who attended church together regularly. Still, though, to do his duty as the family's spiritual advisor, and to put his mind at rest for once and for all, Reverend Temple knew he must pay a call to the household.

As the minister approached the Teeds' two-storey, yellow clapboard home at 6 Princess Street, he was only mildly apprehensive. After all, his own experience with such domestic upheavals told him that, if there was a problem in the home, it would be of a practical nature. Initially, Temple's confidence increased when Daniel Teed greeted him at the door and ushered him into the room traditionally used for somewhat informal visiting—the kitchen.

Once inside, Temple could see that the shoemaker did not look well. He was pale and drawn. Circles darkened the skin under his eyes and he had lost a noticeable amount of weight in only a few days. And where was Teed's sister-in-law, Esther Cox, the supposedly afflicted girl? Temple began to get edgy. He wondered what sort of situation he was walking into.

A quick look around the room that Daniel's wife usually kept neat and orderly did nothing to allay the visitor's discomfort. Utensils and paper were littered about. A bucket of water, drawn from the outside well, had been left on the kitchen table. This was not only unusual, but outside the community's accepted standards of sanitation. Reverend Temple hoped his reaction to the surroundings was not apparent. He was there, after all, not to judge Mrs. Teed's housekeeping habits, but to bring comfort to a troubled family.

Accepting Daniel Teed's wave of the hand toward an empty chair at the table as an invitation to be seated, Temple nodded and lowered himself onto the hard seat. He was barely settled when a strange noise, almost a bubbling sound, came from the offensive water bucket. Temple swung his gaze toward the sound. At first, he couldn't believe his eyes. It actually looked as though the water inside the rough-hewn container was moving.

That's impossible, he thought as he stared at the liquid. Seconds later, the water in the bucket on the table, nowhere near any source of heat, began to boil furiously. Reverend A. Temple, the Teed family's spiritual counsellor, fled the house in terror. The Methodist minister never returned. But the evil spirit that caused the water to boil spontaneously stayed for nearly two years.

This bizarre paranormal tale began in September 1878, when nineteen-year-old Esther Cox accepted a date with a man named Bob McNeal who worked with her brother-in-law, Daniel. To say that the outing did not go well would be an understatement. McNeal drove Esther in his horse-drawn buggy to a secluded spot outside the town limits. There he tried to have his way with the girl. When she refused to cooperate, he threatened Esther at gunpoint. Fearing for her life, she fled.

Once safely home, Esther headed for bed. She could never tell anyone what had happened, she was sure. The horrible experience would remain her dreadful secret forever. Perhaps by morning, some of the intensity of the awful memory would have diminished and she'd be better able to cope. For now, all she wanted was to pass into the only oblivion available to her—sleep. She crawled onto the straw-filled mattress she shared with her sister Jane and pulled the covers up.

Sadly, Esther's attempt to escape her problems failed, for she slept fitfully at best. Equally horrible images were in her unconscious and conscious minds. The poor girl couldn't even tell whether the object she felt crawling around her, inside the covers, was real or imagined. She kept silent and still, alone in her torture.

The next night was no better. Esther's mind was full of haunting images and something gave every uncomfortable indication that Jane and Esther were not alone in the bed. It wasn't until Jane shrieked that Esther knew the sensations she was suffering were not a figment of her imagination. Jane not only felt and saw a snake-like movement under the covers, but she also heard a scratching sound coming from under the bed.

Leaping from the bed, the two huddled together in fear for a moment before Jane pointed out that, in all likelihood, a mouse had worked his way into the box of quilting squares the girls had stored under their bed. Together, they pulled the box of material out into the open. As they knelt to rummage through the pieces of cloth, the carton rose from the floor and rotated, top to bottom, in mid-air. The cotton contents fluttered prettily to the floor in a silent, brightly coloured display of ghostly power.

Jane's screams woke the rest of the household, and Daniel Teed came running. He laughed at the sight that met his eyes and told the girls to tidy up the mess, get back to bed and not disturb him again. In case these two silly young women were not aware, Teed needed his sleep. He had to work the next day and, to make matters worse, the shop was short-staffed. Bob McNeal had not been at work for two days and no one had been able to find him.

The following night, however, Daniel Teed did not laugh at what he found in the girls' bedroom when Jane's screams again woke him. Jane stood beside the bed, one arm covering her eyes, the other extended toward the bed where her sister still lay. Both Daniel and Jane knew that it was Esther lying on that bed only because it couldn't be anyone else. Nothing about the teenager was recognizable. Her body had levitated from the bed, it was swollen into hideous disfigurement and the exposed skin had turned a horrid, unnatural shade of red. Daniel screamed for his wife to join him. As Olive entered her sisters' bedroom, Esther's body suddenly deflated and fell back onto the bed.

No one could bring themselves to speak of what they had seen. Not only did they not want to frighten the others, but they were also afraid that such talk would somehow make their worst fears become reality. Each of the four suspected that Esther had become possessed.

Their suspicions were confirmed by the end of the week. Sheets, quilts and blankets rose from Esther and Jane's bed and stayed stationary for only a moment before apparently throwing themselves across the bedroom and landing on the floor in the far corner of the room.

Out of desperation and fear, they called in the town's most respected citizen, Thomas Caritte, the local doctor. He administered a strong sedative to Esther. Blessedly for the tormented young woman, the drug induced a deep sleep. The other members of the family were not so fortunate. Whatever had possessed Esther seemed even more agitated that she was unconscious. Inexplicable sounds emanated from the roof and the walls of the house. The noises were loud enough that the neighbours heard them, which spoiled the Teed family's plan to keep their troubles secret. Soon the whole town knew that something was very frighteningly wrong at 6 Princess Street. People began walking blocks out of their way to avoid passing the Teed home.

To make matters worse, Daniel Teed was too haggard from all the commotion to go to work. His family was

suffering from his lost wages and his employer was anything but sympathetic. After all, the shoe factory was now
short two workers, for Bob McNeal had still not shown up
for work.

Hours after being sedated, Esther began to regain consciousness and, when she did, she had a terrible tale to tell.
Bob McNeal had tried to attack her. In an attempt to
enforce his demands, he'd even held a pistol to her head. At
least now, those involved realized that there was a connection between the two mysterious events in the town. Exactly
what that connection could be was still unknown.

Once the sedative had worn off, Esther was able to confirm her drugged mutterings.

"Bob McNeal's spirit must be causing all of this," Jane
Cox declared. As soon as the last word was out of her mouth,
the family clearly heard three bangs on the bedroom wall. It
was as if the evil spirit was answering Jane's statement. If the
manifestation could hear and understand, then perhaps it
would be possible to communicate with the evil and drive it
away. The terrified little group worked out a system, a code of
taps. If the unseen force banged on the wall once, it meant
"no," two taps would mean "possibly," and three would mean
"yes." Still, despite their coded attempts at communication,
they were unable to rid the house, or Esther, of the evil entity.

By the time days had turned into weeks, Daniel Teed
was forced, for the sake of the rest of the family, to send
poor Esther away. Just as arrangements were being finalized,
Esther contracted diphtheria. As she lay in enforced isola-
tion, suffering from this highly infectious and dreaded
disease, the supernatural acts stopped completely. Could
they dare to hope that the situation was over?

As Esther began to recover from her illness, the sight of her familiar surroundings brought back horrible memories of how she'd suffered with the cruelty of whatever it was that had possessed her. It was agreed that she should recuperate in Sackville, Nova Scotia, where another of her married sisters lived. While she was gone, Esther's life was peaceful. Perhaps the horrors were behind her. Even the Teeds' little house, which once echoed with ghostly bangings, was at peace. Feeling that life could finally get back to normal, Esther returned to Daniel and Olive Teed's home in Amherst.

As soon as she arrived, the spirit began playing potentially fatal games with phantom fire. Balls of flames danced about her bedroom and lit her dresses on fire. "Are you trying to burn the house down?" Jane shouted at the invisible arsonist. "Tap, tap, tap," came the affirmative reply. Fearing for their lives, the family once again sent Esther away. A local restaurant owner took the banished girl in and paid a high price for his kindness. After his business had been damaged by increasingly strong poltergeist activity, he too sent Esther away.

A group in St. John, New Brunswick, offered to take Esther in. They were not concerned about the poor woman's well-being but merely curious about the supernatural activities that seemed to follow her. As if out of spite for their ulterior motives, the presence was eerily dormant.

This rest break from her tormentor, combined with her hosts' interest in the subject matter, gave Esther a chance to assess and even discuss her recent horrible experiences. She explained to the people who were giving her room and board that three spirits had taken up residence in her body.

One was that of Maggie Fisher, a former schoolmate who had died. The other two entities were male—one Esther didn't know, but the other, whom she called Bob Nickle, was thought to be the poorly disguised soul of her attacker, Bob McNeal. Unfortunately for Esther's peace of mind, the people who had taken her into their home for such selfish reasons soon became bored with her and they too sent her away.

Meanwhile, the Teed house was quiet and Daniel Teed did not feel he could risk a return of the chaos that had accompanied Esther, so he found a family willing to take her in as a domestic aide. The arrangement worked well except that Jane and Olive missed Esther. They convinced Daniel to let her come back. She did, but not to stay. No sooner was Esther Cox back in the yellow house than the thumps on the walls and roof began again. She didn't even have a chance to unpack her belongings.

The next family to take her in threw the anguished girl out when their barn mysteriously caught on fire and burned to the ground.

By that time, Esther's plight and the bizarre state of affairs in Amherst had made headlines around the world. Among those whose attention was attracted was an American magician. Walter Hubbell proposed staying in the already crowded and tumultuous Teed home in order to exorcise the spirit that had possessed poor Esther's body and, by extension, her life and the life of her family.

Hubbell travelled to the Teeds' afflicted home. On the morning of his arrival, there was a violent rainstorm. The hopeful magician knew, seconds after stepping over the threshold, that he was up against a powerful enemy. As the

Teeds watched in terror, the man's umbrella was ripped from his hands by an unseen force. A kitchen knife flew through the air directly at the newly arrived guest. He ducked just in time and the weapon missed its target, embedding itself in the wall behind Hubbell. Furniture began to move and the bangs that the family had worked into a communication method with the spirit began pounding madly.

The magician's intentions or his arrival, or both, had clearly infuriated the poltergeist. Apports—strange objects of unknown origin—began appearing in the home, while other objects, mundane ones such as a sugar bowl, disappeared. Hubbell likely knew he was into something well beyond his understanding. One thing he did understand intimately, however, was how and why to draw a crowd. These ghostly high jinks could bring in paying customers and make him a tremendous profit, the show-man was sure. He proposed turning Esther and whatever possessed her into something of an amusement park sideshow. Reluctantly, Esther and her family agreed to the man's plan. But the spirit clearly wanted no part of this commercial scheme. In show after show, in town after town, Esther Cox sat on an empty stage, dressed in a bizarre costume—amid complete peace and tranquility. The spirit was silent.

Hubbell began to rely on trickery. Soon objects were flying about Esther as she sat centre stage, but it was clear to even the most naive witnesses that Hubbell had merely perpetrated a hoax. Eventually, audiences stopped showing up and the man made plans to move on to other, hopefully more profitable, endeavours.

Before he left, whether out of kindness or because he didn't want anyone else to be able to profit from Esther's situation, he took her to a community of neighbouring Micmacs. A medicine man from Pictou, Nova Scotia, succeeded where European medicine, magic and Christianity had failed. Esther Cox was finally cleansed of the manifestation that had inhabited her.

Hubbell, not content to let his experiences be completely profitless, published a book entitled *The Great Amherst Mystery*. People were fascinated. The volume sold well for years and served to make the profit the man had initially been after.

As for Esther, she died in her early fifties, having married and become the mother to one son. The source of the horrors she suffered for over a year and a half had never been found or confirmed.

This old but exceedingly well-documented ghost story has become a staple of folklore in the Maritimes. Those who've related it over the past decade or two have seemed fascinated that a Canadian Tire store occupied the property on which the haunted house once stood. The connection between the two is really very weak, for the ghost was clearly a poltergeist and such manifestations are always associated with people, not places. If people were looking for the potential of flying tires, for instance, they were doomed to disappointment and, anyway, the tire store moved on to more spacious accommodations some time ago.

To me, what is considerably more interesting than the more recent use of the land on Princess Street is that Bob McNeal was never seen again. It seems plausible to me that the incident that began the mystery—the rendezvous between Bob and Esther in September 1878—might well have ended in either a murder or a suicide. Perhaps Esther Cox was able to turn away the pistol that McNeal was using to threaten her and she murdered him, or perhaps after Esther had fled, McNeal realized the implications of what he had just done. No longer able to live with himself, and already in a secluded spot, he fired a lethal shot into his own body. Either way, the reason Bob McNeal never reappeared at the shoe factory, or anywhere else that anyone knew of, was that he was dead before Esther Cox even reached her home that horrible evening. It was McNeal's angry spirit that haunted or possessed the body of the woman he once tried to harm.

The Grandfather Clock

Ghosts seem to be more closely connected to some objects than to others. Sources of mechanical power, especially timepieces, for instance, are prone to being haunted. My other ghost story books contain stories of inexplicably stopped or started clocks and watches. The following example of this phenomenon, with a delightful twist, occurred in Winnipeg, Manitoba.

The timepiece involved is a grandfather clock that had been a favoured possession of an elderly man. As the eldest son in his family, he had inherited it from his father and deeply cherished it all his adult life. At the very second that the man died, the pendulum on his treasured clock abruptly stopped swinging.

After the man's funeral, the family set about putting his house in order. One of the first chores to attend to was having the man's grandfather clock repaired. The family took the heirloom to a skilled clockmaker, but the craftsman was not able to find any reason the mechanism would have stopped working. There didn't seem to be anything wrong with it. Unfortunately, he could not get the clock to work again either. As there were no male heirs to pass the stately timepiece on to and therefore maintain family tradition, the clock was brought back to the man's house. His widow simply enjoyed it as a piece of nostalgic furniture.

One day, sometime later, the woman returned home and was shocked to find the pendulum of the grandfather clock, which had been mute and still for so long, swinging to and fro in its case and creating the long-ago familiar sound of loud ticking. As the woman stared at the instrument in disbelief, her phone rang. The voice on the other end of the phone line was that of her son-in-law. He was calling to tell the woman that her first grandson had been born just fifteen minutes before.

Close Cousins

Lydia and David, both in their early teens, were cousins so emotionally close that the bond between them was more like that of best friends or brother and sister. This closeness existed even though Lydia lived in Saskatchewan and David in Quebec. They spent many summer vacations together and kept in touch throughout the year with letters and occasional phone calls.

The events I am about to relate occurred in the summer of 1986. It was one of the years when the cousins were not able to be together over the summer. Lydia was attending a family reunion, but, sadly, David wasn't going to be able to join the group. The teens hadn't seen each other for three years. Worse, when David had phoned to chat, Lydia had missed his call because she'd been at camp.

Fortunately, both had other summertime activities to distract themselves from missing one another. David would be visiting a lake near his home and, now that she was back from camp, Lydia was looking forward to visits from relatives and moving in to a new, larger bedroom in the basement of her family's home.

The day her family's company was to arrive, Lydia spent time making sure her new room looked as nice as it possibly could. In a somewhat unfocused way, she was enjoying the task when suddenly she was jolted by a discomforting image. In her mind's eye, the girl saw a blurred image of her cousin David. He was wearing a very distinctive pink shirt, but that was not the most remarkable feature of the sight. David's hair was billowing out around his head as though being blown about by a strong breeze. Although the image stayed with her for only a few seconds, Lydia was chilled by it. Something about the mental picture was eerie and fore-boding.

I'll have to write to David soon, she thought and then tried to bring her concentration back to what she had been doing.

By early evening, when the guests started to arrive, Lydia had succeeded in pushing the odd vision from her thoughts. It wasn't until the phone rang at 9:00 that her mind began to race. She somehow knew the call was con-nected to her experience a few hours before.

Sadly, Lydia was right. At exactly the moment that she had seen the distorted image of David's face, hair streaming out from his head, he had drowned. He had been wearing a pink shirt over his swimming trunks. Lydia had been in Saskatchewan. David had been in Quebec. The bond between the two cousins was so strong that his spirit had come to her at the moment of his death.

Caged Spirit

In 1877, William Kirby published a novel called *The Golden Dog*. The plot is a grimly romantic one, set against actual historic events. Amazingly, more than one hundred years later, the book, in a somewhat abridged form, is still in print. It offers a raw and colourful glimpse into life in Quebec City during the mid-1700s. *The Golden Dog* also provides a dramatic description of a ghost who, legend has it, still haunts Old Quebec.

The sight of this haggard spectre is not one that any witness could readily dismiss. In life, Marie-Josephte La Corriveau proudly declared herself a witch. If true, her actions proved that she was a vicious one. La Corriveau had been suspected of being involved with a murder by poisoning before eventually being convicted of a second one—the murder of her husband. According to Canadian historian Frank Anderson, she killed her husband "by pouring molten lead into his ear while he slept."

In 1763, the year that she committed her heinous crime, La Corriveau was promptly charged with "Petit Treason." On April 10, the woman was executed in a gruesome manner.

According to the closing paragraphs of Kirby's book, the convict was "gibbeted" (an archaic term for being hanged) inside an iron cage. Even after she had died, humiliation awaited the woman. The cage, with La Corriveau's rotting corpse still inside it, was left on display for passersby to gawk at.

Not surprisingly, the indignity to her body seemed to cause restlessness in La Corriveau's soul. The murderous witch's ghost, still encased in the iron cage, was reported to chase after people who paused to gawk at what remained of her mortal self. Eventually, officials of the church heard about the terrifying apparition that had pursued and frightened even normally calm, credible parishioners. Arrangements were made for an exorcism to be performed. The first ritual was apparently unsuccessful. A second, and then a third, attempt at the rite were performed, but according to William Kirby, the manifestation "dragging her cage at her heels" persisted, "defying all the exorcism of the Church to lay her evil spirit."

Those horrid ghostly sightings, and even the phantom's pursuits of terrified mortals, went on, undiminished, long after La Corriveau's caged, decomposed body had been taken down from the spot where the execution took place and (still encased in the metal confine) had been buried. Some sixty years later, a farmer "digging in the earth" had the misfortune to "discover the horrid cage, rusted and decayed." In a truly bizarre twist, once the death trap was recovered, it was sent to an American museum. As no further documentation exists to prove that the ghost of Marie-Josephte La Corriveau continued to haunt Quebec City, it would be interesting to perform something of a ghostly census at the museum where the relic was shipped to. I wouldn't be surprised if the place suddenly had great difficulty keeping guards on staff!

Author Val Cleary, in his book *Ghost Stories of Canada*, recounts this story with additional drama. Because that anthology, published in 1985, is generally catalogued as fiction, it's probable that Mr. Cleary wanted only to be entertaining, not misleading. In the interests of presenting as many aspects of this legendary Canadian ghost story as my research has turned up, I offer the following.

After interviewing Romeo Dionne, apparently one of Marie-Josephte's descendants, Cleary wrote that the deceased's caged body remained on display "for more than fifty years." According to this colourful version of the tale, the cage was eventually claimed by members of the woman's family who then sought to profit from their ancestor's crime and suffering. Dionne claimed that the cage still existed, that he knew where it was and that the ancient, rusting mesh was possessed by La Corriveau's angry spirit. His proof? The evil device had been indirectly responsible for at least two deaths.

The first death had occurred in the 1870s while the cage was on display. During a windstorm the cage, which was suspended from the ceiling of the early-day exhibition hall, began to swing about wildly. A metal edge of the contraption hit a kerosene lamp, which started a fire. The flames engulfed the area so quickly that a man nearby was killed in his sleep.

The next victim of the ghastly, ghostly murdering spirit, Cleary suggests, was Dionne's own grandfather, who was found in a storage area on his property. His nearly lifeless body was pinned under a pile of scrap metal that had fallen from its precarious stack. Resting on the very top was the rusted, evil cage. The old man died less than an hour later.

Considering that this ghost story originated in the 1760s, and was not recorded in written form until the late 1870s, it isn't surprising that the tale has developed variations. What is both surprising and interesting is that this ghostly piece of Canadiana haunts us into the twenty-first century.

Phantom Footsteps

With the help of a dear friend, I was able to collect some fascinating, first-person accounts of hauntings throughout Canada's eastern provinces. The Landrys were one couple who responded with a description of their paranormal encounters in 1990.

Angeline Landry wrote about a poignant incident. "My husband and I were living with my parents in the country [rural New Brunswick]. One night at approximately 1:30 a.m., the whole family heard someone walking on the porch with heavy work boots. My brother slowly went down the stairs to see who it was. Nobody was there and the footsteps stopped. We all decided to go back to bed."

The family's attempt to rest was short-lived, for as Angie further explained, "Minutes later, the footsteps started again. This time, my husband, my brother and I started to go down the stairs to see who it was. My brother, being the tough guy, decides to go outside on the porch and see for himself. The porch is an 'L' shape (along the front and side of the house). He comes back in, says no one is there. Again, we all go back to bed. This happens one more time and then it stopped."

After sleeping through the rest of the night, the family reassembled in the morning. "We all spoke about it ... how weird [the experience through the night] was."

Later that same day, their misgivings and wonderings were given a sad answer. "My husband [Chris] heard about an accident [that happened] about a thirty-minute drive from where we were. A man driving a small car in the early morning, approximately 1:30, crossed the [centre] line on the road and was hit head on by an oncoming truck."

It was later determined that the car's driver had died instantly.

Angie continued, "That man ... was a good friend of my husband's family. They say the spirit tries to find someone close to them ... [in this case] that 'someone' was my husband. Those footsteps we heard that night [sounded like] the way this man walked. A sluggish walk with heavy boots, that is exactly what it sounded like when he walked."

All who had heard the phantom footsteps then realized that the spirit of Chris Landry's friend had passed close by them on his way to the great beyond.

A few days after my communication with Angie, I spoke directly with Chris himself and he explained that, as a child growing up in Moncton in the 1960s, he'd had experiences with the supernatural.

"It started as far back as I can remember, when my brothers and sister were friends with a woman who was using a Ouija board. Weird things would happen when they were doing a séance and people would get nervous. They would stop and the glass [they were using as a pointer] would fly off the table and smash. One night, they were doing a séance and my mom was in the other room. She didn't know what was going on. It was about midnight. There was a vase of water [on a stand]. She had taken the flowers out of it and there was just the vase full of water left. It lifted up off the television stand, the water all poured out and then the vase came right down in front of her."

Chris added, in classic understatement, "She freaked out."

This story was not an isolated incident for the Landry

family. Chris explained that the ghost has "been haunting us all of our life, from one place to another."

Their history has left the Landrys convinced of the existence of spirits, and that may have played a part later when the accident victim decided to visit Chris as his soul was passing on.

Mistaken Identity

The Landry family's various paranormal encounters are described earlier in this book. Bob Landry was kind enough to share the following story as well.

Bob Landry recalled an especially stressful time for his family during the Second World War, the winter of 1942 to be exact. "My brother, Gerry, a mechanic, was in the Air Force. He and another man were on mercy flights in the north with a bush pilot named Al Cheesman. They were flying on a mission to deliver medicine to some northern people when they got lost. Their plane went down and they were lost for thirteen days."

During this time of terrible worry, the Landry family tried to keep going as best they were able to. Mrs. Landry, for instance, kept up with her housework.

"My mother had waxed the floors and it was snowing so she put newspapers over them. About midnight, we heard the front door open. We could hear the squeaking of the frosted hinges and then we heard someone bang their feet on the floor, as if to shake off the snow. Then we heard footsteps coming up the stairs and someone knocking—three heavy knocks. My sister and my father went downstairs" to see who had come in.

"There was nobody there. There was not one drop of water on the newspapers. They looked all through the house. They went out and looked on the front porch and there was about a foot of snow but no footprints in the snow. I remember my mother saying 'That's Gerry asking for prayers, probably dead and asking for prayers.'"

Deeply saddened, the family turned in for the night. The next Sunday, as was their habit, the family went to church.

Bob Landry recalled, "The priest had asked all the parishioners to pray so that the searchers would find Gerry, or at least find the remains, if they had been killed. The following morning we got a call from a fellow at the Air Force Base who knew the family and who knew Gerry. He said they'd just got word on the wire that they'd found Gerry and the other two. They were on a lake somewhere in northern Quebec. He said, 'They can't come out today because it's storming but all three of them seem okay. One of the guys had a broken leg. He was on a stretcher but Landry and Cheesman were okay and now the [searchers] have their position.'"

This news immediately wiped away the sorrow they had felt after hearing the ghostly footsteps throughout that eerie, snowy night.

"We were all happy. We called up some friends and relatives to come celebrate. They went to the liquor store and got a bunch of stuff. They were drinking, having a happy time and cheering the fact that Gerry had been found alive and well. That's when a knock came on the door. It was one of the parish priests, Father Clarence. He asked if we were related to a certain man, that they had found his body. He died Saturday night. This man was an alcoholic and he was living alone. My mother had helped him many times. She made him promise to go to church."

It took a while before the family was able to make sense of what had happened. The phantom footsteps that they'd attributed to Gerry's soul had, in fact, been that of the family friend.

"We figured out later it was [the ghost of] that old guy. He wanted a burial because, when the priest came he said, 'We don't know what to do with the body—should we just bury him in the back of the cemetery or what?'"

Because Bob's family had cared for the man during his unfortunate life they also offered to take the responsibility for his well-being after death.

"We said, 'We'll give him a funeral.' In those days they didn't have funeral parlors like we do nowadays so the casket was brought in to the front room. Where we had celebrated the finding of Gerry we were now in the presence of a corpse because [the deceased] had come so strangely that Saturday night to ask for a burial."

The ironies of life—and of the afterlife—can be poignant.

River Wraith

Stoney Rapids, Saskatchewan, is roughly equidistant from the eastern and western boundaries of the province and just south of the most northerly boundary. Even though it is prime hunting territory, at least one experienced hunting guide conscientiously avoided the area—particularly the banks of the nearby Porcupine River—after a series of experiences during the fall of 1939.

Claude Arteaux had been guiding in the region nearly all his adult life, having learned the skill by accompanying his father on expeditions with hunting parties. They were both familiar with the local legend of "The Lost River Wraith" but neither really believed it—until a particular hunting trip. Once Claude encountered the phantom, the experience changed him forever. He never again set foot on the surrounding soil, and he developed a healthy respect for the awesome power of the supernatural.

At the moment he heard the horrible, ghostly sound, Claude Arteaux was standing by himself. His father and another man were roughly 1 kilometre (0.6 miles) away on the riverbank. Claude later described the ear-splitting noise as a "shriek-like wailing." The sound startled him to the core. Cocking his rifle in preparation to shoot, Arteaux made his way, as silently as he was able, toward the river where the sound had seemed to originate.

At first, he could see nothing except his father and the other man. They were standing on the riverbank—as still as could be. Claude called out to the men, but, rather than giving an answer, the elder Arteaux merely pointed to a spot over the river and slightly above his head. His son followed the angle until his eyes focused on an eerie-looking cloud of vapour.

"Don't come any closer," the older man warned. "Turn away." His blood seeming to turn to ice water in his veins, Claude assented and, as he did, the details of the legend flooded through his mind.

The so-called River Wraith was supposed to be the ghost of a murdered man. It was rumoured that a person who saw this phantom would die within a year. *Such foolishness*, Claude thought, as he heard his father's footsteps coming closer and closer to him until the older man touched him on the shoulder and urged him, "Come on, let's get out of here."

The three men made it safely back to camp, but did not discuss the ghost sighting. Three months later, Claude Arteaux's father, a man of fifty-two years of age who had been in perfect health, became fatally ill. Just weeks after that, the man who'd been with Mr. Arteaux on the riverbank also died suddenly and, in this case, under mysterious circumstances.

Frightened and grieving, Claude began to discuss the strange "coincidences" with his friend Roger Leclaire. Perhaps in an attempt to comfort the troubled young man, Leclaire pronounced that the legend was nothing more than a silly, meaningless tale that had somehow survived. To prove his point, Roger Leclaire announced that he would set out in search of the wraith on Porcupine River.

Roger Leclaire never returned from that hunting trip— a ghost-hunting trip. His body was found several days later in the river, its facial muscles contorted and paralyzed into a horrible grimace—as if the last thing he'd ever seen in his life had frightened him to death.

Ghostly Queen

Bill and BJ, a young couple from Fairbanks, Alaska, arrived at Dawson City, Yukon, one June evening in 1962. It had rained all day, and by the time they made their way down Dawson's main drag, they were cold, wet, tired and broke. Their moods were as dark as the mud puddles that formed along King Street. Determined to find some protection from the downpour, they crawled under an old dilapidated building, unrolled their sleeping bags and drifted off into the relief of sleep. They might even have slept throughout the night except that they'd unknowingly chosen to bed down beneath a haunted theatre.

Bill was awakened first, thinking he'd heard the sound of sobbing. Worried that BJ wasn't well, he lifted his head and strained to hear. It wasn't BJ because, by then, she'd also woken up. She was fine, although concerned, because she too could hear the weeping. The sounds were so disturbing that Bill took his flashlight out and shone it around the crawl-space they were lying in. He couldn't see anything but, by that time, they could both feel vibrations from the floor above them. It sounded as though someone was walking across it. Soon, both the sounds of sobbing and the footfalls ceased and the pair of not-very-happy campers fell back to sleep.

Less than an hour later, the young trespassers were awakened again—this time to the echoes of laughter, conversation and honky-tonk tunes. The sounds seemed to come from a long way off and yet be right above them at the same time. Whichever it was, they'd heard enough. Bill and BJ fled into the wet night with a story to tell their grandchildren.

Too bad the couple hadn't known that the ghostly sounds they were hearing were completely harmless—merely remnants of the past, energy from the theatre's glory days, recorded in its atmosphere and occasionally replayed.

There's almost no doubt that the spirit of Kathleen Eloisa Rockwell—or "Kate, Queen of the Klondike"—was responsible for the phantom weeping, but she may also have contributed to the party sounds. Even a cursory investigation of the theatre's history explains her continuing presence there, through the deterioration, demolition and eventually reconstruction of the building that had been so much a part of her life.

Legend has it that, in the very early twentieth century, Kate was a popular chorus girl in the Yukon. She became involved in a relationship with theatre magnate Alexander Pantages. After Kate supplied him with most of the money to build the Dawson City show place, Pantages broke Kate's heart by leaving her for another woman. Despite her sorrow, the woman lived to the age of eighty, dying in 1957. In death, the former Klondike Queen's spirit returned, almost immediately, to haunt the theatre she'd helped build.

Not many weeks after Bill and BJ's ghostly encounter, the original building was torn down and replaced with an exact replica, built on the same location. Throughout all these stages, Kate's presence has remained. Painters and carpenters working on the reconstruction reported seeing what they described as "a very pretty lady" suddenly appear on the stage. She stared at the workers for a few moments before "disappearing into thin air."

Parks Canada runs tours of the theatre and at least one guide, Jane Olynyk, has been aware of the ghostly presence. On a Monday night in August 1976, Jane was locking the place up for the night. Part of that routine involved making sure that no one had stayed behind in any of the theatre's seats. Toward this end, the woman made her way to centre stage after turning on the "house lights" to illuminate the auditorium. That was when she first saw Kate's apparition. The ghost wasn't menacing. She was simply standing on the left side of the second balcony.

The sighting didn't frighten Jane, who knew the folklore about the ghost and recognized the image from archival photographs she'd seen of the woman known as "Queen of the Klondike." If the ghost's flamboyant gown, combined with the distinctive red hair, weren't enough proof of the haunting, the fact that the image Jane saw was ever-so-slightly see-through certainly would have been.

Moments later, the manifestation began to walk away. It looked back, smiled down at Jane, and then vanished. The sensitive and accepting tour guide felt warmed by that particular encounter but other times she could feel the deceased woman's great sorrow. This sensation, Jane reported, was an all-encompassing one that she could not help being affected by.

Although not everyone is as sensitive to the ghost's presence as Jane was, Kate's spirit is widely accepted as being in the theatre. Most people associated with the place feel that the ghost is a guardian of sorts and enjoy her continuing presence.

"Devil Dog"

On a warm July day in 1983, three brothers—Bim, Rupen and Depen Pandya—set out to go camping with their friend Rob Sosteric. All four young men were excited about the trip, especially as only Bim had ever been camping before. Driving away from their homes in Regina, the four were sure that the trip would be both fun and memorable. Little did they expect that it was to be a trip they'd puzzle over for the rest of their lives.

En route to Lake Diefenbaker, they stopped for lunch in Saskatoon but hurried through the meal. They had so much planned and were eager to get to the campground.

By 4:30 in the afternoon, the carload of happy campers was pulling up in front of the campground's store and office. Rupen and Bim piled out to pay the registration fee and to choose the best available campsite. On the way into the building, the teenage brothers passed a big black dog sitting in front of their car. As the animal ignored them, they ignored it and neither mentioned it at the time.

While those two were in the office, Rob got out of the car to make a phone call from a payphone. Rob too saw the large black dog and noted that it was right in front of their car. Again, the dog didn't seem to notice him so Rob didn't think anything more about the animal than the other two had.

Depen, the youngest boy, was left alone. He got out of the car, intending to join the others but, oddly, as soon as his feet hit the dusty parking lot, the dog that had been sitting perfectly still for several minutes "started to go crazy," according to Rupen's description offered some seventeen years after the incident occurred. Not surprisingly, Depen quickly decided that staying alone in the car was safer than risking the unpredictable behaviour of a large dog.

None of the four boys gave the black dog's presence, or its inconsistent behaviour, a second thought as they found their campsite and began to pitch their tent on what Bim knew was a prime location at the edge of an inlet.

The boys then set out to pump up their little dingy so they could get out on the water. Surprisingly, they had trouble. No matter how hard any of them tried, they could not get air into the raft. They decided to take the dingy to a service station with a high-pressure air hose. The trip was a success, but it meant the inconvenience of driving back to the lake while hanging on to an inflated raft balanced atop the roof of the car. They had run out of time to use the raft that day but looked forward to the fun they'd have with it the next day.

Perhaps feeling just a tad smug about tenting among all the tent trailers, campers and recreation vehicles around them, the young men began preparing dinner. Later, the four campers sat by their roaring fire until nearly midnight. Once tiredness and a sudden increase in the wind finally forced them into the tent, the boys sorted out which one of them was to sleep where and then, in true camping tradition, told one another spooky stories before falling asleep.

At roughly 2:00 a.m., Rupen was awakened by strange noises just outside the tent. Forcing himself fully awake, he concentrated, trying to identify the sounds. *Was something rustling on the ground? A mouse perhaps?* He thought it might be a voice that he was hearing—a voice calling for help. *Surely my ears are playing tricks on me,* he thought, but as he continued to listen, his concern mounted. Not only was Rupen sure he could hear the words "help me," but the voice seemed to be moving closer and closer to the tent.

Not knowing what else to do, Rupen awakened Rob, who did his best to talk his friend out of the thought that he could hear a voice. As their conversation heightened, it woke up both Bim and Depen, who mumbled inquiries as to what was happening. Rob replied, "Your brother's hearing ghosts." Everyone laughed and lay back down, totally unaware of how prophetic that teasing statement was.

Rob, Bim and Depen were soon fast asleep again, but Rupen did not seem to be able to drift off. Roughly half an hour later, he was still wide awake and sure he could hear the voice again. This time it was even clearer. The words were "help me," the voice was that of a child, and the tone of the voice was, as Rupen later described it, "very pathetic."

It was also very puzzling. Why had there been no sound when his brothers and Rob were awake with him? Rupen tried to console himself by deciding that, when all four of them were awake, they were simply making too much noise and therefore couldn't have heard such faint sound.

The next time Rupen heard the voice calling for help, he decided to investigate. Grabbing the axe they'd brought for splitting firewood, he made his way outside as noiselessly as possible. The wind had died down considerably, but the plaintive cries for help were becoming stronger. That was enough for Rupen. He went back into the tent and woke up Rob again. As soon as the other boy opened his eyes, Rupen signalled him to be quiet and listen. And that was when Rob first heard the disturbing words "help me, help me."

Convinced that someone needed assistance, the two boys who were awake shook the two who'd managed to sleep through the disturbance. After Bim listened, as ordered by his younger brother, he ventured that the voice might be from "a little kid in trouble."

Why would such cries go on for so long, they wondered? Were they some kind of a sick prank? Despite their misgivings, the boys knew that they could not ignore the plaintive pleas.

Panning the area with a flashlight, Bim and Rupen crawled out of the tent. As the light beam bounced off the trunks of the trees surrounding their tent, the boys suddenly caught sight of something moving. Shining the flashlight in the direction of the movement, they were jolted to see the same large black dog that had behaved so strangely the previous afternoon. The animal simply walked out of the bushes, "calmly and as if he had been waiting there," Rupen recalled, before adding "the voice stopped and the dog walked off toward the lake."

The boys climbed back into the tent, trying to convince themselves that the dog had somehow made the noises they'd heard. Although all four boys tried to fall back to sleep, no one was able to and, a couple of hours later, they began to pack up their site. After their eerie experience and virtually sleepless night, they decided to spend the next night in a Saskatoon hotel room.

Try as they might, the four could not get the ordeal of the previous night out of their minds. The events were the topic of many unanswered questions. "If the cries 'help me' were a prank, then why did they go on for four hours? Where did the 'devil dog' [as they had begun to think of the strange, black animal] come from? Why did the dog show up at our campsite which was all the way across the highway and a bit of a drive from where we first saw it? Why hadn't any of the people in the other campsites been drawn out of their beds by the noises?"

The next day, on the final leg of their trip back home, the three brothers and their friend heard a radio news broadcast about a man and his young son who had drowned in Lake Diefenbaker the day the boys had arrived there. The victims had been accompanied by their pet—a large black dog. The animal had survived the mishap by swimming to shore.

Rupen, Depen, Bim and Rob listened to the news in stunned silence. Could they have somehow heard the ghostly echoes of the little boy's final cries? Was it that child's dog that they'd seen? If so, was the animal attempting to protect Depen because he was a young boy just like the dog's now-deceased owner? Was that why the dog had barked at the child when he'd attempted to get out of the car? Perhaps the tragedy was even connected to their difficulty with the raft. Had something been trying to prevent them from getting out onto the lake? Had the dog been sitting in the bushes guarding the boys to make sure no further fatalities occurred?

Today, the brothers and their friend who shared this bizarre encounter are all adults. None of them, however, has forgotten that disturbing night in the campground, and their questions about the experience have never been answered.

Lady In Pink

The next story is the kind Hollywood movies are made of   with one important difference. This story is true.

Because the residence in question is now a rehabilitation centre, I shall leave the property unidentified except to say that it is located on a large piece of land nestled in the Laurentians. Despite the haunted building's enormous size ("five living rooms, eleven bedrooms, a billiard room and a massive dining room with a big oak table that would sit twenty people"), the place was, before being given over to institutional use, owned and occupied privately.

It wasn't long after moving in that Larry suspected something of a paranormal nature was at work in the house. "The dining room was particularly chilling for me, as if that was one room where I was not welcome."

Fortunately, his own private space in the house gave him a very different sense.

He wrote that his own bedroom, on the second floor, was 14 feet by 34 feet (4 metres by 10 metres) with large windows on three sides. Although not all rooms gave him the negative feeling that the dining room did, he soon realized "the only place I really felt alone and welcome was in my bedroom."

A bit of research into the history of the house made that safe feeling somewhat surprising because as Larry learned later, it was in that room that "the mistress of the house had died."

Larry explained that once all eleven bedrooms had been rented out and the house was, therefore, fully occupied, he and his roommates decided to celebrate by hosting "a massive, black-tie party." The formal soiree was well planned and so, by late on the day of the gala, there was really little to do except relax until the guests arrived and the festivities began.

"While we were waiting for the guests to arrive, one of my partners and I were in the billiard room. It was early evening," Larry began.

As the pair chatted, something just outside one of the windows caught their attention. It was "a woman, standing in the cul-de-sac of the driveway in front of the house. She was wearing a distinctive, off-the-shoulder pink evening gown," Larry described. "We waved and she waved and [then] she went in the front door."

Realizing then that the party was under way, the two men left the billiard room and went into the main part of the house. They didn't see the woman in the pink evening gown but didn't give that any thought. After all, a large number of people were gathered in a large house. One party-goer could easily mingle for several hours without meeting everyone present.

The house-warming extravaganza was a great success. Guests and hosts enjoyed themselves equally. The party went on for hours and it wasn't until the next morning, when Larry and his friend were, once again, alone together, that either of them thought about the lady they'd seen approaching the house so many hours before—the one wearing the "pink, off-the-shoulder gown." After some considerable discussion, they realized that, although they had both watched her come into the house, neither one of them had seen the unknown female after that.

The mystery had them intrigued. They began to contact a few of their friends and ask if anyone else had seen this woman. Surely at least one person who'd been at the party must have known who she was. No matter how many people they asked, no one else seemed to know who the distinctively dressed woman was. Nor could anyone even remember seeing such a person. Larry and his friend were stumped.

It wasn't until "a few months later," when they were investigating parts of the house they'd previously not explored, that they came up with a possible explanation for the disappearing guest.

"In one of the closets, we found a picture wrapped in brown cardboard and tied securely. When we opened it up, [we discovered] it was a painting, a painting of the woman we had seen in the driveway. She was even wearing the pink dress."

The mystery guest, whom no one else had seen and who had disappeared upon entering the house, was the same woman whose likeness stared back at the two men. She was the home's former mistress, the woman who had died in the bedroom that now welcomed and housed Larry. Finally, their mystery was solved. They'd long known the house was haunted. Now they knew by whom, but no one was ever able to determine why her restless soul continued to roam about.

Foreign Phantoms?

Jerry encountered his first ghosts in the fall of 1970. He firmly believes, and for good reason as you are about to read, that these phantoms were responsible for saving him from the Grim Reaper. But Jerry had already been saved at least once, having survived active duty during the Korean War of the early 1950s.

After his military service, Jerry chose to live away from Canada's metropolises. He became a trapper and prospector in the Yukon. It was an isolated existence but an adequate one, and he always had his team of dogs for companionship.

On one of his treks with the dog team, Jerry was making his way through the desolate scrub-brush countryside near Pelly Crossing, a community close to the confluence of the Pelly and the Yukon rivers, approximately 275 kilometres (170 miles) north of Whitehorse. The footing is treacherous in that area. Moisture-retaining mosses grow thickly along the ground and, where there are dips and hollowed-out patches, this circumstance creates dangerous footing— muskeg. Such a bog is almost impossible to get through as it sucks down anything pressing on top of it. Each footstep taken across that surface becomes more and more difficult until people attempting to traverse the terrain either find their way out or collapse from the sheer exhaustion and are effectively trapped.

On that cold, dark autumn night, Jerry was very close to collapse when he happened upon a slight rise in the ground. It was not a large area of elevation but there was sufficient space for him and his dogs to rest. He would be able to build a fire and stay there for the night. Come morning, with the daylight, Jerry was confident that he'd be able to find his way to firmer ground.

Once he had a fire burning strongly, Jerry was able to cook a basic meal. The dogs hungrily licked up his "leavings." With that bit of nourishment, the warmth from the impromptu hearth and his utter physical exhaustion, the trapper was soon asleep.

Some time later, he was awakened by the dogs yelping and jumping up against their harnesses. Jerry sat up and started to speak to the nervous animals. He couldn't imagine what might have disturbed them, but he was sure the sound of his voice would calm them. He didn't even have time to utter a sound before his voice was taken away by the shock of the sight before him. There, less than 2 metres (6½ feet) before him, stood five people—at least they looked like people. He knew right away that the figures he was seeing four adult men and one teenage girl—were actually apparitions.

For a moment, the ghosts and Jerry simply stared at one another. Then one of the male presences spoke. Jerry immediately recognized that the language the spirit spoke was neither French nor English—and yet, to his amazement, he understood each word the image said to him. The ghosts were clearly angry with Jerry for being where he was. He was intruding, they let him know in no uncertain terms before vanishing as mysteriously as they had appeared.

Badly shaken, Jerry climbed back into his bedroll, but he had not been able to fall back to sleep before the ghosts appeared once again. This time the spokesman's tirade, still in an unidentifiable language that Jerry somehow understood, was so severe that the girl in the group appeared to try to quell her fellow spirit's anger. Her attempts were not effective. Jerry became very afraid. The strength of the phantom's anger seemed to be increasing. Not knowing what else to do, Jerry shrieked obscenities at the presences. The spell was broken and the images disappeared again.

Jerry knew that he would not be able to sleep again that night, but he lay back down to rest. Before long, the animals began to whimper. He looked up, expecting to see that the ghostly gathering had reassembled but, much to his surprise, the only entity in front of him was that of the young woman. He called out a greeting to her image and she answered him in her strange language. The wraith explained that she knew Jerry would have difficulty finding his way out of the dangerous bog unless he followed her instructions. And then she was gone.

The trapper lay awake until daybreak, but the ghosts never reappeared. He broke camp at first light and, following the explicit directions the girl had given him, made his way clear of the bog.

Days later, Jerry and his team made it back to their

cabin, never understanding what had occurred on the muskeg that night, except that, once again, the Korean War veteran's life had been inexplicably saved.

Possessed Plane

In the early 1990s, an aviation buff was killed as the huge helicopter he was piloting crashed in the southern Yukon. In addition to all the usual matters that need to be attended to after a sudden death, his grieving family also had to dispose of the deceased pilot's collection of airplanes. The family decided to entrust the job to an auction company that specialized in aircraft sales.

A Calgary resident named Clive bought one of those planes, "a Piper J3 Cub dating from the late 1940s." Of course, at the time he made the purchase, Clive had no way of knowing who the plane's previous owner was or that he had died in a plane crash. He was just pleased with the purchase.

"I got it at a good price because it needed a bit of work done on it," Clive explained before adding that he'd "been an aircraft owner for a number of years" and looked forward to repairing his newest possession despite the possibility that finding parts "for a fifty-year-old airplane" might be a challenge.

The pilot's apprehensions turned out to be unfounded. The restoration process went, in eerie retrospect, smoothly. Clive stored the plane with another one he owned at a small airport in Airdrie, just north of his home in Calgary.

One day, in February 1992, not long after he'd completed the work on the vintage aircraft, Clive received a phone call from the people at that airport's administration office. They needed to report that some "strange things had happened. The J3 Cub had somehow taken off, flown over to another row of airplanes and landed dead centre on our other plane." This activity had occurred even though the plane had been "thoroughly tied down, each wing and the tail were tied down."

Clive did not keep his caller on the phone long. He and his wife dashed out to the Airdrie airport where they were met "by one of the three people who had seen all of what had gone on. All three of these people were other aircraft owners and mechanics."

The witnesses were shaken by what they'd seen. They offered to walk to the scene of the strange event with the plane's owners. True to his colleague's description, "here was one plane upside down on another."

Approaching the planes, Clive was fascinated and puzzled to note that the planes were extremely precariously balanced. "The rudder of the J3 was sitting on top of the rudder of the other craft, an area about half an inch (12 millimetres) wide and both rudders are rounded. If they weren't dead centre, give or take half a millimetre, one would've slipped off the other. I couldn't believe how totally dead centre the one was on top of the other."

Clive knew, in the natural world, what degree of pilot finesse would be required to pull off such a landing. For

Piper puzzler—who flew the plane?

an apparently invisible pilot to accomplish this act was more than he could fathom. Concerned that the balancing act would not be maintained through the winds that were expected in the area that night, they decided to tie the plane in place and deal with its removal the next morning.

As they made their plans, "a 3-mile (5-kilometre) an hour wind came up and pushed the rudder of the one plane down and it went clunk and so now at least we could tie them together more easily."

Before the group of aviators had a chance to collect tie-down ropes they "noticed that this antique J3 Cub was now lifting straight up, straight up from [the back of the other plane]."

These experienced people were definitely confused by what had happened so far, but the most puzzling event was yet to come.

The Cub "rapidly accelerated, heading south. It was still upside down, by the way, and went into an amazingly steep climb. One of the pilots commented that even with the biggest engine in them [such planes] normally couldn't climb like that J3 was climbing."

Some very unusual force was undeniably at work here. The plane "got up to somewhere around 100 metres [328 feet] above and 100 metres south of the airplane it had been on top of and then ... did a perfect half loop, came down, did a 100% perfect, three-point landing, taxied up and stopped about 2 feet [0.6 metres] from the plane it had been sitting on."

In complete shock and disbelief, the group "just stood there with mouths open."

"My God, there's no pilot in that thing. How could it do this?" one of the witnesses asked rhetorically.

Evening was setting in by this time and it was too dark to do much more than just tie the plane where it had landed and deal with the unnerving problem the following morning. They began to move a car in place to use as an anchor for the errant airplane.

Clive remembered, "Nothing happened till [the driver] put his car to the front of the plane. They started to tie it down. It was getting dark and one of the others said he'd have to be going home."

"I'll give you a drive," offered another man but, as he "put his hand on the driver's door, he felt the car move." The pair looked up to see the possessed plane "hovering right above."

It took a long time for these people, even though they were familiar with all sorts of aircraft, to figure out what was happening. The restored Piper J3 Cub "was behaving like a powerful helicopter."

After "many other weird things happened with that plane," Clive decided to research its history. That was when he discovered that the haunted Cub had once belonged to the pilot who had been killed when his "powerful helicopter" had crashed in the southern Yukon.

The deceased pilot's spirit had, apparently, not been ready to leave his love of flying behind.

Laura's Legacy

For several years, at least a couple of times each year, I presented a writing course to aspiring authors. Periodically, former students would contact me. Some had additional questions to ask, some had publishing success stories to share, and some, like Laura, were kind enough to share their own personal ghost story with me. Her story is dramatic.

Laura began relating the encounter as though it were a child's sad fairy tale. "Once upon a time," the young woman wrote, "in an apartment long ago, lived a thirteen-year-old girl who was just told her father was dead."

She continued, "The year was 1973 and we had just returned from a disappointing month in Great Britain."

Laura's mother, Ruth, had raised Laura as a single parent and had planned the move to Britain to be permanent, but "the situation in Britain was a financial nightmare. Feeling that this was an inappropriate environment to live in," Ruth chose a new place to live in by sticking "a pin in a map of Canada" and accepting its choice of their future home.

The mother and daughter team were "depressed and lonely," Laura explained, when they landed in Toronto to, once again, start life anew.

They adjusted reasonably well to their new home and had been living quietly in an adequate apartment in a central area of the city for some time, when Laura's birthday rolled around. Coincidentally, that day, relatives contacted Ruth to let her know that Laura's father "had died in a dreadful camping accident."

Not wanting to spoil her daughter's special day, the woman delayed sharing the news. When Ruth did tell Laura about the death, the girl's emotional reaction was limited because she had only "one vague memory of meeting him," and Laura acknowledged that "feeling something was a stretch."

At the time, Laura had no way of knowing that her father, who'd had so little to do with her when he was alive, was, in his death, about to profoundly affect her existence.

She began to explain, "My first memory of a 'problem' around our home started while I was sitting on the couch watching the local TV news. It was mid-winter, cold, and Mum was in the kitchen making supper. She came in [and] sat for a moment while the dinner cooked. As the local newscaster boomed out the horrors of the world events, I saw a 'pinwheel' roll across the living room carpet—and through the wall!"

Startled by the sight, Laura glanced at her mother. "Did she see this spirit wheel too? I summoned the courage to ask, 'Did you see that?' She answered, 'Yes.'"

The haunting had begun.

Although Ruth and Laura's apartment was small and their resources limited, the pair had a pet. Percy was a cat with a lot of personality. Ruth did not have her own bedroom, but slept on a fold-out couch in the living room. Each night as she began to make her bed, the cat would play on, under and around the sheets. The game became part of the bedtime routine.

Describing her mother's nightly ritual, Laura explained, "After the game, she'd settle in and turn out the lights." Unfortunately, that was when another "unwanted 'game' began. My father's ghost [would] pace back and forth in her hallway area. He appeared like a streak of black—fast moving and frightening. Mother would summon her courage and say, 'George! Stop it!' The black would disappear. As the weeks progressed, my father became more insistent on 'attention' as we figured his motive [to be]."

Neither mother nor daughter had any ideas as to what to do about the haunting. "We were lost," Laura stated flatly. Despite their poverty and their ghost, the pair tried to make the best of their lives.

"Our apartment was decorated with old mismatched furniture and the walls were pretty bare. One day Mum found a cheap picture, minus a frame, for one of our walls," Laura described before adding, "I managed to save up my allowance to buy some, then-popular, black light posters."

Laura continued, "Then the fun truly began. Mother would find the [frameless] picture ... on the floor, on its side. Nothing seemed to be disturbed on the route to the floor and the nail was still in the wall. A few nights later, she came home from work to find the picture down again. Over and over this happened until one fateful day mother said aloud, 'Just once I'd like to see how that happens.'"

Ruth had not long to wait. Laura recalled that one evening, some days later, "Mum was curled up with a good library book and, on a break for a gulp of tea, she lifted her eyes." It was then that the woman "saw the picture come away from the wall, drop down a foot to just above the items on the chest it hung above, then pause ... slide to the left without touching anything and then slam to the floor."

The incident astonished Ruth and badly startled Percy

the cat, who "had been asleep under a table." To add to Ruth's feelings of discomfort, the animal "came out to stare at something near the picture." Although Ruth could not see what the animal evidently did, the cat's eyes "followed as if watching someone walk across the room. Both my mother's hair and the cat's were standing on end by then!"

Percy was also implicated with the ghostly encounters that began in Laura's bedroom. "I discovered [that] Percy liked to bat at the posters on my wall, leaving little tears, so I began to make it a habit to shoo him out of my room and lock my door when I went out. After one evening out, I returned to my room and, as I opened my bedroom door, all nine of my black light posters slid off the wall, into the centre of the room, in precise military-style timing. I stepped back in horror. The room was icy cold. I could easily feel a presence and I didn't like it."

Ruth was sure the entity in their apartment was Laura's father's spirit, and his intensity was increasing. One night, as an invisible force pulled the woman's bedding off, Laura, who was in bed in the next room, was terrified by seeing an image of a "hideous vision ... a headless man swinging from the ceiling, as if hung from a rope!"

Feeling completely terrorized and utterly helpless, the pair began to seek help. They approached a traditional church where the congregation "offered prayers and doubted our sanity."

But Ruth persisted. "One day my mother looked through the Sunday papers and announced [that] we were going to a Spiritualist church. They talk to the dead."

Convinced that there was a chance this non-traditional

form of theology could help, the pair made their way to the address given in the newspaper. Laura was much more skeptical than her mother was and, as they made their way to the church, the youngster kept warning her mother to be very careful not to give away any information that a charlatan could manipulate.

"Little did I know that they [the spiritualist congregation] would instantly blow my mind. The subway ride took longer than we expected and we got to the church late," Laura recalled. Their arrival did not go unnoticed.

Laura described the scene as they settled into the church. "A woman in a purple dress said, 'I'd like to talk to the little girl and her [mother] who came in late.' She then described my father in minute detail and gave information that I didn't know. She accurately described his height, colouring, the way he died and the fact that one side of his face had been hideously scarred."

The mother and daughter were badly jolted by the confirmation of their worst fears, but at least it might have prepared them somewhat for what was to follow.

"The incidents around our apartment were getting worse and worse. [For] over a year and a half we suffered my father's activity. He rattled pots, put an ice-cold ghostly hand on visitors' shoulders and chased them away. No one wanted to visit and potential boyfriends disappeared in a hurry. One favourite trick was 'Hide the Margarine Container.' It disappeared from the fridge for two to three days at a time and then 'arrived' back in a closet."

The ghost proved that he liked to play practical jokes. "My mother took to wanting a bit of something sweet after lunch and began going downstairs in her downtown Toronto office building for a chocolate bar."

Ruth liked a particular chocolate bar with a creamy centre. But one time when she bought the candy, "the creamy centre had turned to solid chocolate. My Mum showed [it to] a co-worker thinking it was a manufacturing mistake. 'Hey, look at this—they messed up at the factory!' The other secretary laughed and suggested that she write to the company. 'Maybe you'll get a free bar!'" Laura's mother just laughed at both the strange occurrence and her colleague's advice before eating the chocolate bar.

"A few days later, the same urge for chocolate occurred. Mum went through the same thing [but] this time mentioned it to the sales clerk. The woman patiently explained that such a thing was 'impossible' as these chocolates came through a mechanical processor and could not get through quality control in such condition. My Mum shrugged, bought the same creamy bar and went upstairs. Again the bar was solid chocolate."

This time the co-worker who'd been so quick with the advice before, "nearly fell over." She told Laura's mother, "That's impossible, Ruth! You have to take that back this time."

Laura continued, "Mum decided the clerk downstairs needed to see the quality-control goof and wrapped up the bar. She followed the twisting route down to the store and found the clerk. 'See!' she said, proffering the bar."

Much to both women's amazement, "the creamy goo oozed out over the foil paper. My mother stood open-mouthed and embarrassed. The clerk backed up—probably deciding Mum was the local 'nut' and my mother cursed out my father all the way back to her office."

The ghostly pranks with food had only begun. "Mum bought a can of green beans, at least that's what the label said. When she opened the can to heat them, [she found] lima beans inside."

Ruth took the can back to the store and received a similar lecture about the impossibility of such a thing because of the standards in a food-processing plant.

By now, the almost-constant presence of Laura's deceased father and his ghostly antics had become too much for the pair to endure. When both of their favourite rings disappeared from separate jewellery boxes, their patience came to an end.

Laura explained, "We contacted a man who was noted (though very quietly) for 'rescue work.' He would go into a trance, contact the spirit and ask what this was about. He would channel the spirit's anger or guilt and let it get it off its 'chest.' Then, the spirit would 'feel' relieved and leave. This gentleman got all the facts about the case and said that he and his group would begin by praying together for guidance. The next morning, I went next door for a loaf of bread to make a sandwich and 'something' took ahold of me and shoved me deliberately down the stairs and into a restaurant [where] I had been once before. 'Okay, okay,' I muttered. 'Don't shove.'"

In the restaurant Laura met a psychic whom Laura has chosen to call "Lynn." An interesting conversation developed as Lynn asked, "So, who's the tall, skinny man beside you? Black hair, blue eyes?" The woman was describing Laura's deceased father who, of course, was not with her—not in body, anyway.

At that point in her re-telling of the events, Laura wrote, "What followed ended the haunting and secured my belief in the supernatural forever."

Lynn and Laura left the restaurant together and went directly to the haunted apartment, determined to make every effort to "cleanse" it once and for all. "Lynn was asking for support and wanted to know if there were any people who could assist us .... We called the woman pastor of the spiritualist church we had been going to. [We] also called Mum. It was impossible to get help from either source."

The women were on their own, resolved to help the spirit of Laura's father leave his earthly ties. In a word, they needed to "help" him. Once that thought was in place, a plan unfolded.

They decided to have a séance in the apartment to perform an exorcism. "The area [of the apartment where the séance would be held] was to be secured in white. Everything in the circle must be white. The circle must be sealed with white candles and salt. No one shall leave the circle until the exorcism is finished," Laura described.

The cat, Percy, was "locked into the bathroom with his litter box. Percy disliked this situation intensely and wanted everyone and all spirits to know this [he clawed at the closed door and made loud and persistent vocal protestations]. His noise went on until Lynn fell into a trance. She was lowering her head as she was 'overtaken' and, as she did this, the scratching and meowing from the bathroom ended abruptly. Was the cat harmed?"

Laura's question was rhetorical for, at the time, she couldn't have known how the cat was. She had to stay involved with the supernatural process around her—

a process that seemed to have taken on a life of its own.

"[Lynn] channelled during that day with pure light streaming in from the windows. What I saw did not fit any explanation I've ever heard of trickery or manipulation. Frankly, I would tempt fate by putting the same circumstances in front of any magician and bet my life they could not do what she did!"

Laura explained that Lynn's "head lifted and [she] became 'it' unequivocally. One eye stared straight ahead and the other rolled in an outer circle. She cussed worse than any sailor."

Laura readily acknowledged that nothing in her life had prepared her for this moment. An evil-looking entity that had taken over Lynn's body informed the pair that George was in purgatory—"not exactly hell, but a place of confusion." Shortly after that statement, the being left Lynn's body and she awoke from her trance.

Laura described the changes in the apartment's atmosphere. "The cat immediately began to scratch and meow. Was the timing a coincidence?" Unfortunately, she could not risk breaking up the session by going to check.

"As the exorcism went on, we had the same type of thing happen over and over. The cat, the silence, the [entity]."

Not surprisingly, Laura was shocked by the evil force coming through this woman she had just met. "I bantered with nasty responses, 'Dad deserves peace. Why don't you let him free?'"

"Ha!," Lynn's body said, "You don't know what he's done!"

"No," Laura replied, "but I know some of his story and I know he still deserves peace."

"Why?" the evilness challenged.

"Because he's a human being," Laura countered.

"WAS a human being," it howled back.

This eerie conversation continued until Laura "finally asked to speak to my father. There was an argument about this but it [the evil entity within Lynn's body] finally allowed this. An angel of some sort was sent first, then, as my father appeared [he] angrily apologized. When I said it was 'OK' he roared, 'Not you—your mother!' Apparently Dad felt guilty about the promises he made to Mum and never kept. I assured him [that] she forgave him and he took a breath. A black puff of smoke popped out of Lynn's body in her abdominal area and floated toward the ceiling."

Laura reported that she observed that phenomenon "in utter amazement."

Not knowing what else to do, Laura "waited for Lynn to recover." While the medium returned to herself, "the cat started up again and we did a final prayer for Dad. It was then [that] we noticed that hours had gone by. It was near dinner time and [yet] the [lit] candles had not burned down at all. It was as if the room and circle were protected and the candles were some kind of a symbol of the unearthly power present. The air in the room now smelled different ... springtime fresh."

For Laura, though, the most important change was that she "felt peaceful."

As the eventful day was winding down, Laura's mother arrived home. "We recounted the unbelievable story to her. She too noticed the difference in the room." Laura and her mother gave Lynn dinner to thank her for all her trouble. Then, Lynn "left and we never saw her again. She did us a great service and I will never know if Dad put her there or just saw her and knew she could help. Perhaps Lynn was the angel! I'll never know."

As is so often the case with stories of life as we actually live it, Laura's amazing anecdote did not tie up as neatly and tidily as a piece of fiction surely would have.

"We never got our favourite rings back and frankly I felt angry about that one point. I always wondered where they went. Were they being worn by a spirit somewhere? Are they in the limbo of nothingness that the margarine container hung in? If so, how does one manifest them back into existence?

"After all of this ended, Dad seemed to send the final signal. A few short months later I received a letter from my father's mother (for the first time in my entire life). She wished me well in my forthcoming marriage and sent me a cheque for $500. I was engaged, but how did she know? And ... how did she suddenly get the money to spend on me? What made her write? Was it Dad keeping the promise he made to Mum years ago, [a promise] of money?"

Not being able to answer any of her own questions did not detract from the intensity of Laura's reaction to the gift from beyond. "I was in tears and I still believe it was Dad sending a final gesture."

In closing, Laura acknowledged, "I'm aware of how odd this story is to others who have never been touched by the occult and its odd experiences. Whatever is thought of what I have told you—it is the truth. And, somewhere in the universe there's a father, a mother and two favourite rings—all a part of this."